MODERN WITCHCRAFT FOR BEGINNERS

YOUR COMPLETE GUIDE TO WITCHES, WICCA, SPELLS, RITUAL MAGIC, DIVINATION, COVEN, TRADITIONAL AND CONTEMPORARY PATHS

FRANK BAWDOE

MODERN WITCHCRAFT FOR BEGINNERS

Your Complete Guide to Witches, Wicca, Spells, Ritual Magic, Divination, Coven, Traditional and Contemporary Paths

Frank Bawdoe

© Copyright 2021 - All rights reserved.

It is not legal to reproduce, duplicate, or transmit any part of this document in either electronic means or in printed format. Recording of this publication is strictly prohibited and any storage of this document is not allowed unless with written permission from the publisher except for the use of brief quotations in a book review.

Disclaimer: Any medicinal benefits given here are a product of my own research and as such should not be taken over the advice of trained medical professionals. Always make sure that anything you consume is 100% safe. If you are pregnant, consult your doctor or midwife before consuming something you haven't tried before.

 Created with Vellum

CONTENTS

SPECIAL BONUS! — 9
Introduction — 11

1. WHAT IS WITCHCRAFT? — 13
   Wicca and Witchcraft Origin — 15
   Modern Wicca vs. Traditional British Wicca — 16
   Common Myths and Misconceptions — 19
   Eclectic Wicca — 22
   Dianic Wicca — 23
   Seax/Saxon Wicca — 23
   Celtic/Druidic Wicca — 24
   Shamanism — 25
   Animism — 28
   Alchemy — 29
   Church of Wicca — 29
   Finding the Right Coven — 30
   Steps for Starting a Coven — 32
   Coven (the Wheel of the Year) — 33
   Samhain: Halloween — 35
   Yule: Christmas — 36
   Imbolc: Candlemas — 36
   Ostara: Easter — 37
   Beltane: May Day — 37
   Litha: Midsummer/Summer Solstice — 38
   Lughnasadh: First Harvest — 38
   Mabon: Thanksgiving — 39
   Hermetic Order of the Golden Dawn — 40
   Choosing a God or Goddess — 40
   Worshipping and Working with a Deity — 42

2. HOW TO LEARN MAGIC IN THE MODERN WORLD — 43
   What is Magic and How It Can Help You? — 43
   Collecting Magical Energy — 44

Magic and Modernity	45
Bringing Technology into Magic	46
Finding Your Magic Place	48
Frank's Boost Your Intuition Spell	49
Daily Passive Magic	50
Speaking to the Nature of Spells	51
Controlling Your Energy	53
Modern Magical Energy	56
3. DIFFERENT TYPES OF WITCHCRAFT AND WITCHES	**59**
Modern Witchcraft	59
Genetic Witchcraft	60
Kitchen Witchcraft	60
Humanities Witchcraft	61
Criminal Witchcraft	62
Grandmotherly Witchcraft	63
Ethnic Witchcraft	66
Seidr/Norse Witch	68
Georgian Witch	69
Sun Witchcraft	70
Moon Witchcraft	71
Star Witchcraft	72
Storm Witchcraft	73
4. WITCHCRAFT SUPPLIES AND THE WITCH'S COMMON TOOLS	**76**
Sacred Spaces	76
Altars and Shrines	77
Magic Wands	79
Athame	80
Witch's Bell	80
Besom	81
Candles	81
Cauldron	83
Salt	84
Charging Daily Items	84
Opening and Closing a Circle Ritual	88

5. HERBAL MAGIC FOR WITCHES ... 90
   Essential Herbs ... 92
   ALOE VERA ... 92
   ALLSPICE ... 93
   ANGELICA ... 93
   BASIL ... 94
   CARAWAY ... 94
   GINGER ... 95
   CINNAMON ... 96
   MINT ... 96
   STAR ANISE ... 97
   Incense ... 98
   Frank's Incense Recipe ... 99
   Magical Powers of Trees ... 100
   Magical Power of Flowers ... 103
   Frank's Rose Petal Beauty Lotion ... 106

6. STEP BY STEP GUIDE TO RITUALS AND CRAFTING SPELLS ... 109
   Intention ... 109
   Invocation of Hecate (The Goddess of Witchcraft) ... 111
   Crystal Magic ... 112
   Meditation ... 114
   Mindfulness ... 115

Final Thoughts ... 117
Sources ... 121

SPECIAL BONUS!

Thank you for adding this book to your Wiccan Library! To learn more, why not join Frank's Wiccan Community and get this additional Free Wicca Starter Kit Book 100% FREE!

Hundreds of others are already enjoying insider access to all of my current and future full-length books, 100% free!

If you want insider access plus this Free Wicca Starter Kit Book, all you have to do is **scan the code below** with your smartphone camera to claim your offer!

INTRODUCTION

Do you want to become a witch? Do you want to understand the history of witchcraft, the intricacies of the different paths the pagan world offers, and to delve into what it means to practice witchcraft in the modern world/age? Reading this book, you will learn the differences and similarities between Wicca and witchcraft and Paganism and witchcraft, the difference between solitary and coven witchcraft, and you'll understand the history and founding of the modern Wiccan religion and its influences. The Wiccan religion is dedicated to the betterment of humankind. To Wiccans, magic is real and exists on the Earth. Through modern-day witchcraft and ritual, tribute is paid to nature, the elements of Earth, Wind, Fire, Water, and Spirit and reverence is given to the two deities, the Moon Goddess and the Horned God.

In reading this book, I am looking forward to you gaining an understanding of the fundamentals of witchcraft and its many incarnations, what it means to choose the spiritual paths of Gods and Goddesses, along with ways to practice holidays and rituals. Furthermore, I expect you to become familiar with the rich history of traditions based on ancient pagan beliefs, learn how to cast circles, and practice calling the quarters and elements.

As a devoted spiritualist, Frank Bawdoe shares a deep-rooted fascination with the philosophy of Wicca and Paganism. With a sincere desire to help people of all races, genders, ages, and cultural backgrounds to embrace spirituality, the magic of witchcraft, and to discover the divine within themselves, Frank is driven to ignite the flames of emotion in readers who are passionate about exploring the essence of life. Frank Bawdoe has authored numerous books on Wicca and Paganism, including *Wicca for Beginners* and *Witchcraft Religion & Spirituality and New Age Divination*. A passionate seeker of spiritual knowledge, Frank has explored paganism and Wicca in-depth with unwavering faith and dedication for truth.

In this book, Frank explores the history, theory, and practice of magic in the Wiccan and pagan cultures through the use of spells, meditation, visualization, and intuition, with the goal of transforming lives and finding harmony with the Universe.

Through magic comes serenity, a relationship with your higher-self, and an understanding of the common misconceptions about Wicca and witchcraft in general. You will be provided with accurate and up-to-date information about the fastest-growing religious practices in the world and learn common ritual tools used in magic, the different kinds of witches, and magic practices. You will learn how to craft your spells and rituals with several example spells provided. Learning divination and sigil magic is a way of infusing a pattern with magic that directs it in a prearranged way that can direct specific actions for those who know how to cast them properly. All magic is based on the techniques of meditation and mindfulness.

1

WHAT IS WITCHCRAFT?

WITCHCRAFT IS A NATURE-BASED AND VIBRANT PRACTICE IN spirituality that is alive and kicking in our modern times, just as it has always been throughout history. It is also a topic of cosmic proportions that can be overwhelming for those just starting out. There are many perspectives and much to learn about the best methods, techniques, and the correct ways to practice magic. This is one of the more complex studies of all forms of religion and spirituality. However, lighting some candles, buying some crystals, and burning midnight essential oils are only a few of the tools that witches use on a regular basis when practicing their craft. Of course, you don't have to take my word for it because there are over a million Americans and almost 100,000 Britons currently practicing some form of paganism that you can ask!

There is a plethora of types of witchcraft and many choices for a new witch to pursue. Rather than overwhelming you with information, I think it's helpful to become familiar with some basic terms below:

Paganism: Paganism is an eclectic term for religious practices other than the Christian, Abrahamic, Islamic, and Judaic faiths that emphasizes the spiritual aspects of earth and nature. Neo-pagan is the term for modern-day practitioners who typically follow a spiritual path through life that is based on seasonal cycles, nature, and astronomical patterns. Some pagans refer to themselves as polytheists because they honor more than one deity. One of the many otherworldly paths falling under the representation of paganism is the religion of Wicca.

Wicca: Wicca is a more popularized form of the neo-pagan religion attributed to a large degree to the named Father of Wicca, Gerald Gardner. During the mid-1900s, Gardner cultivated this form of paganism now known as Gardnerian Wicca. Whereas historically witches were usually thought of as only women, there are many men Wiccans who worship both goddesses and a god. Originally, Wicca was deemed as anti-monotheistic. It has recently come under scrutiny for favoring heterosexuality and the concept of a binary gender. This, in the 1970s led to the rise of Dianic Wicca, for witches who only want to worship the triple goddess and to only conduct rituals with other females. Since then, this particular train of thought was proven to be troublesome, due to many covens prohibiting transgender women.

Ceremonial: This is a practice followed to a T, or by-the-book, so to speak, where rituals, spell work, and ceremonies are executed according to traditional Gardnerian Wicca. Most often, ceremonial witchcraft is considered to be a highly preparatory and complex form of magic. The use of special occasion clothes, along with single-use tools fills a ceremonial atmosphere with seriousness.

Brujería: Brujería is an umbrella term for witchcraft practiced by Caribbean, African, and indigenous Latin Americans, with a history going back thousands of years. The word bruja is Spanish for witch.

Solitary: These witches have chosen not to participate in a coven, but rather operate in their own mix or type of witchcraft of their choice.

Eclecticism: These witches have chosen a more social path and have chosen not to adhere to a specific category of witchcraft but instead use a variety of traditional methods.

Initiation: This is a group of rites that put newbie witches on their path to becoming official witches. They usually accomplish this rite of passage by joining a particular coven and learning its traditions and practices for the ceremonial year and a day. With enough dedication, experience, and knowledge, these initiates have the opportunity to become a high priest, high priestess, or the leader of a Wiccan coven.

Coven: This is a community or gathering of witches who have been already initiated and are led by a high priestess or high priest. In the Wiccan religion, witches usually meet during Sabbats, which are celebrations known as the Wheel of the Year, and also at Esbats, which are held in observation of a full moon.

WICCA AND WITCHCRAFT ORIGIN

Wicca was a coven-based religion that developed in England in the early 1900s. Its religious exercises were primarily based on the texts of witch groups, such as that of Margaret Murry and other traditional British Wiccans. One of history's most famous Wiccans was born in England in 1884 and was called Gerald Gardner. Gardner was an ardent follower of a witch known as Aleister Crowley, and was a member of a witch group called the New Forest Coven. Gardner then went on to become the founder of the modern-day religion of Wicca. By the middle of 1950, Gardnerian Wicca practices spread throughout Great Britain, Australia, and the United States.

Gardner learned his practice while he was working in Asia. Just prior to WWII, he went back to England and got involved in the local occult community. It was Gardner's Wiccan philosophy that led to people changing the way they thought about witchcraft into a positive perception. Prior to that, witchcraft was often perceived as satanic and barbaric devil-worshipping. Before this time witches were only thought to be women. If a woman stood out because of being sexual, intelligent, or independent, she was accused of witchery, and many women were burned at the stake. If a man was ever associated with witchcraft, he was thought to be a flamboyant homosexual.

MODERN WICCA VS. TRADITIONAL BRITISH WICCA

British Traditional Wicca, much like Gardnerian Wicca, operates as an initiatory mystery cult; membership is gained only through initiation by a Wiccan high priestess or high priest. Any valid line of initiatory descent can be traced all the way back to Gerald Gardner, and through him, back to the New Forest coven. Coven and ritual ceremonies are kept secret from outsiders and many witches of the Wiccan faith choose to keep their membership in the religion a secret. Individual witches decide whether they want to be open or keep their religious affiliation a secret, usually in consideration of where they live, their circumstances in life, and their careers. In every instance, traditional British Wicca strictly forbids any member from sharing personal information and someone's membership status without the complicit consent of that member, for each and every specific time of sharing. This is done for the protection of that member from harassment and other heinous acts that may be committed against them. Like those who keep their sexuality closeted, Wiccans often talk about coming out of the "broom closet." In traditional British Wicca, Alexandrian Wicca, and Gardnerian Wicca, there are three types of initiation which seem to be based upon the Freemasonry's three grades: Theology, Ethics and Morality, and the Return of Three.

Gardnerian Wicca Theology

There are two main deities in Traditional British Wicca (TBW), the Mother Goddess and the Horned God. It is a dualistic view of divinity, with God and Goddess regarded as opposite, yet equal celestial forces. A shared core belief held by most Wiccans is the practice and acceptance of ritual and magic. Similar to the viewpoint of Aleister Crowley, Wicca defines magic as the art and science of making change happen in accordance to will. Wiccans believe magic is as natural as nature itself; a manifestation of transformation, not supernatural forces, that involves a combination of meditation, invocations, music, movement, and tools. Wiccans use magic as a tool to enact upon a quantum or energy level of reality. The quantity of energy makes the decision about which direction reality will take.

Alexandrian Wicca

Alexandrian Wicca, named after Alex Sanders, was grounded in Gardnerian Wiccan philosophy. In the 1960s, Alex and his wife, Maxine, began their own branch of Wiccan religion, Alexandrian Wicca. Before a member is initiated, it is decided by the members of the coven as to whether the individual would be a good fit to their coven by gathering in an open ritual to interview the initiate. If accepted, an official offer to join the coven is made, and once the initiate accepts that offer, they start the first phase of initiation without being bound by the coven's vows. This phase usually lasts about a year, during which the initiate is exposed to the elders and the coven. The decision is traditionally made by the matriarchal representative, a high priestess. Once welcomed into the coven, the initiate then makes the decision whether to commit themselves toward a more serious journey, which is achieving the first degree of initiation. As a first-degree initiate, the new coven member needs to exhibit dedication and commitment to learning the craft with great enthusiasm. In the traditions of the Alexandrian Wiccans, every member is a priest or priestess. There are no lay people in this Wicca version; all coven members possess the ability to commune in fellowship with the Divine.

Wiccan Ethics and Morality

Traditional Gardnerian Wicca follows a core guideline of ethics known as "The Wiccan Rede." In a manner of the archaism still presiding in Gardnerian lore, "As it harms none, do as thou wilt," or in modern terms, when using magic, it can never be to cause anyone harm, unless it is to prevent a greater harm. The meaning of the word Rede is "counsel" or "advice." The counsel to harm no one carries equal weight as doing as you will. Therefore, Traditional British Wicca stands strongly against any form or coercion and strongly advocates informed consent. It forbids witches from proselytizing others and requires that anyone who wants to be initiated into the Wiccan religion does so through study, teachings, and requests to be initiated.

The guideline of Wiccan ethics is known as the Rule of Three or the Law of Return. This ethical guideline advocates that any positive or negative energy a person puts forth in the world will be returned to that person three-fold. This ethical boundary exhibits the importance of harming no one, for that would give rise to a harmful reaction back on oneself or on one's coven. These traditional Wiccan teachings inspire thought before action, especially when it comes to spell work. The coven and individual witches adhere to these guidelines as to consider beforehand what possible consequences may come from any magical workings. With respect to these ethical guidelines, it is safe to say that Traditional British, Gardnerian, or Alexandrian Wiccans hold themselves to high ethical standards. For example, the Bricket Wood coven was noted for having many members from intellectual and academic backgrounds and contributing to the preservation of Wicca traditions and practice. Gardner actively participated in disseminating academic resources regarding the occult and Wiccan folklore to the general public by opening his Museum of Witchcraft located on the Isle of Man. Traditional British Wicca differs from some modern-day magical practices that tend to concentrate more on the practitioner's spiritual development.

COMMON MYTHS AND MISCONCEPTIONS

Wicca was legally recognized as a legitimate religion by the Court of Appeals in 1986. However, Wicca is still a widely misunderstood practice and its members are misunderstood as well. Many modern-day witches chose to carry the title of Wiccans because the term "witch" still carries such a negative and evil connotation. One of those commonly misconceived conceptions is that Witches cast spells to harm or curse people. Loosely based on the rites and rituals of paganism hundreds of years ago, the focal point of Wicca is to give reverence to the seasons, magic, and the harvests. The government of the United States of America has ruled Wicca as an official religion, thereby making its holidays federally observed. However, they do vary according to state. In New Jersey, for example, eight Wiccan holidays are celebrated and recognized by the New Jersey Department of Education, allowing Wiccan children to be excused from classes on those days. Wiccans are entitled to the same rights as any other group.

Another big misconception regarding Wiccans is that they are devil worshipers, when in fact, they do not even believe in the idea of Satan. Concepts such as hell and heaven have never been part of the Wicca religion. Wiccans believe in goddesses and gods, not a single God, which is not that different from Buddhism and Hinduism. Likewise, animal sacrifices are a commonly held misconception about the religion of Wicca. Wicca is a nature-based religion and its members have nothing but respect for all living things. Sacrifices offered to Wiccan deities are given in the form of bread, flowers, fruit, or wine. There is no form of blood sacrifice in the Wiccan religion. Many Wiccans are animal lovers and animal activists.

Wiccans do not follow the writings of the Holy Bible, but they have created and handed down a Book of Shadows (BoS) to use only as a reference book. Wiccans are also known to keep magical grimoires (diaries), where they keep and record useful knowledge for practicing their spell work, rituals, and ceremonies. Magic is considered to be a natural activity in life, and Wiccans believe spell work is natural and should be used for various acts of good, healing, personal growth, and prosperity.

Also a misconception regarding Wiccans is that they are sexually perverse. While they consider themselves to be liberal and nonjudgmental in regard to sexuality, it doesn't mean they engage in orgies or bestiality. Wiccan do consider gossiping about who is having sex with whom as trivial, unimportant, and a total waste of time. The only thing that really matters to most Wiccans is informed consent. A person's sexual preference, be it homosexuality, bisexuality, heterosexuality, or pansexuality, is of no interest to Wiccans.

Another common misconception about Wicca is that all witches are female. It is undeniable that the origin of the legacy of witches is based on women, which is because its history has been perpetuated by the demonization of witches and witchcraft to begin with. Witches are like everyone else, they come in all shapes, sizes, colors, genders, forms, ethnicities, and races. Historically, witches were women who were persecuted for any semblance to witchcraft, while men who practiced spell work were revered as magicians and sorcerers. Witches were considered threatening to the patriarchal society because they didn't conform to societal and gender norms.

WHAT IS WITCHCRAFT?

Contrary to some beliefs, people are not born witches. You sometimes hear about some attention-seeking individuals insisting they were born a witch. This can't be true. Magical ancestry is a powerful influence but it has no bearing on whether or not someone is a witch. There are very real aspects of witchcraft. Curses and hexes are real, which is in part the reasoning behind the Rule of Three. However, this rule also applies to positive magic. Hexes are primarily a black magic practice. While many consider white magic to be good, magic is neither evil nor good, it simply is magic, a tool used in spiritual expression. You definitely do not have to have years of training and initiations from confirmed witches in order to cast a spell. To do it, you don't need a full moon, animal bones, or a coven to enact spells. You simply need to put forth your intention and then perform a ritual to manifest that intention, be it a candle lighting ceremony, meditation, or some other form of magical expression.

You can write a letter to yourself with affirmations that you are special and loved and that you honor the Goddesses, God, or deity of your choosing to be practicing magic. Write a gratitude list and make a repeating chant out of it and you are practicing magic by harnessing positive energy; you are casting a spell. You don't have to have a lot of money to do this; magic is not an expensive practice and now that it is seeing a rise in popularity, it has become more accessible than ever. The myth that it is demonic and evil is increasingly being exposed. However, let me issue a healthy warning here. The witchcraft industry is becoming a big money industry, with many scammers looking to cash in on the incense, candle, crystal, and essential oil market. All you need to be successful in spell work is you! You have the power and the energy to make magic; this is never found in an item. You need not belong to a coven because you may prefer to "fly solo." There are also eclectic groups and other less governed witch groups who practice their craft in a more casual setting than covens with highly organized initiation processes. Every person's spiritual journey is unique and personal, so it is really up to you if you want to join a coven.

ECLECTIC WICCA

Eclectic Wicca is an all-purpose form of modern Wiccan practice that doesn't fit into any distinctive category. Many solitary witches choose an eclectic path; however there are covens who identify themselves as eclectic. An individual witch or a coven may identify as eclectic for various reasons including:

- Mixed traditions: A solitary witch or a coven may use a mixture of practices and beliefs from several different traditions and pantheons.
- Modified traditions: A group can be an extension of a traditional established branch or Wicca, such as Alexandrian or Gardnerian, but has been modified in its practices, which makes it very different from the original Wicca tradition.
- Individual and unique forms of practice: A person can create their own tradition of practices and beliefs. Because this form cannot be defined as something specific, it is defined as eclectic.
- Uninitiated witches: A solitary witch may be practicing their craft by what they have learned from sources available to the public regarding Wicca, but not be using initiatory, oathbound materials; hence, their practice is eclectic.

Because there is often confusion about who is and isn't Wiccan, there can be disagreement regarding existing ancestral Wiccan traditions, and modern eclectic traditions. Some would say that covens based on traditional Wicca should be allowed to identify themselves as Wiccan. If we take that reasoning into account, any coven or individual who identifies as eclectic is not Wiccan, by definition, but Neo Wiccan. "Neo Wiccan" is not an insulting or derogatory term, it simply means practicing a new form of Wicca.

DIANIC WICCA

Dianic Wicca started from the feminist movement and was founded by Zsuzsanna Budapest, a hereditary witch. Dianic Wiccans pay very little attention to the Horned God and focus primarily on the Goddess. Hence, most of their covens are exclusively female. A few, yet far between, have welcomed males into their group. In some area, Dianic covens have been stereotyped as lesbian witches, but that is not the case.

While most Wiccan sectors follow a system of beliefs that limit cursing, hexing, or negative magic, Dianic Wiccans are the exception to the rule. The Wiccan author, Budapest, is a known feminist who has argued that binding or hexing those who commit harm to women is acceptable. She calls for, in particular, binding and hexing of any men who have perpetrated violence against women and children. Dianic covens are self-identified, so it is known that their beliefs are Goddess-base, and that they are spiritually focused on feminism. They do celebrate the Wheel of the Year.

SEAX/SAXON WICCA

Saxon Witchcraft, also known as Seax-Wicca is a modern Pagan Witchcraft, largely influenced by traditional Anglo-Saxon Paganism during the Early Middle Ages, between the 5th and 10th centuries. It was founded by Raymond Buckland, a Gardnerian Wicca High Priest born in England in 1934, who then moved to the United States. He had expressed his disquiet about the egotistical, corrupt, and abusive nature of some of the covens he witnessed. To address those concerns, he developed Seax-Wica. He wrote one of the first books, entitled *The Tree*, that explored solitary modern Witchcraft and offered seekers a way to introduce them to a modern Saxon Witchcraft that could either be practiced in a coven or alone. Seax-Wiccans usually honor Freya and Woden, who are Germanic deities, and the eight Sabbats. They use the usual ritual tools, including a spear, and hold rune magic in high regard.

CELTIC/DRUIDIC WICCA

When they hear the word Druid, most people picture old men wearing robes with long white beards frolicking around Stonehenge. However, Neopagan Druidry is a religious philosophy about the ways of living life; while founded in ancient soil, it reaches for the stars. Of all the differences that a Wiccan has with a Druid, this is probably the most prevalent. In Druidism, there is no "Rede." In fact, the only people that the Rede pertains to are those who adhere to it; it is unique to Wiccans and some kinds of witchcraft.

Most Wiccans believe in the adage of "do as you will as long as you don't harm anyone in the process." Some Druids disagree that this ethical guideline has anything to do with them. Some Wiccans even accuse Druids of lacking ethics. However, this is certainly not the case. In fact, the moral virtues within the Rede and the Law of Returns actually imbue Druidism. Normally, Druids refer to this as Celtic Virtues. In general, these morals are described as Honesty, Honor, Justice, Courage, Hospitality, and Loyalty. These are the six principles of Druidic ritual and thought. To put it briefly, the morality of Honor requires one to hold true to their oaths and to do the right thing, even if that means hurting someone else in the process. Druids are obliged to stay true to family, leaders, and friends, defining their virtue of Loyalty. Druids also feel a sense of obligations toward being a good host when visited by friends or family, defining the virtue of Hospitality. Telling the whole truth to your Gods and your fellows adheres to the virtue of Honesty. Druids understand that every individual has inherent worth and that to hurt that worth demands consequences in some form or another. Courage, according to Druidism, means standing strong in the face of adversity alone or with companions.

Outside of the six virtues, pretty much anything goes. The Justice virtue holds you accountable for any harm to others and any good things you do; it's just. It recognizes the divine in each and every one of us. It is a commitment to do good. It is very similar to the Buddhist and Hindu concept of karma. However, this concept has not been part of European thought. The Celts have a history of functioning as an isolated tribal community. The Celts believed in independence as a supreme right, and fiercely demanded that right to be proudly honored.

SHAMANISM

Shamanism is a spiritual practice where the shaman (practitioner) interacts with the spirit realm through higher states of consciousness, such as meditation and trance. The Shaman's goal is often to direct spiritual energies or spirits, usually for healing purposes, into the physical world. Shamanism is not an organized religion, but more of a spiritual practice that cuts across all creeds and faiths, delving into deep aspects of ancestral memory. As a primitive faith-based belief system, it was practiced long before established religion. It has its own cosmology and symbolism, inhabited by totems, beings, and gods who share similar characteristics, while depending on their set origins, appear in various forms.

Shamanism has been practiced and studied in cultures around the globe since the times of ancient people up to the modern day. The shamans' work is adaptable and practical and has coexisted over thousands of years with varying systems of government, organized religions, and cultures. Formalized religions, from Christianity to Buddhism, are rooted in ancient shamanism and still carry the shamanic traits of a strong connection to the divine in all things. However, shamanism itself is not a formal ideology or belief system, but a group of experiences and practices shared by shamans around the world in every culture. These adaptable practices coexist with different governmental systems, organized religions, and various cultures.

Nowadays, shamanism is practiced and studied as a life path. Following the perspective of shamanism, people look to be in a relationship with the spiritual aspect in all things. They find guidance and information for alternative realities for their own experiences in life, intentionally. Shamanism doesn't inherently contradict the practice of religion that allows an individual to be directly involved with whatever they choose as a power greater than themselves. Today, as was in ancient times, people consult with shamans for pragmatic and practical solutions to everyday problems, including healing illness, family discord, career challenges, and ancestral issues.

Shamans practice in enraptured or elated trance states, voluntarily, which transforms their consciousness for astral travel through the invisible realms. The ability to effect changes and gather information in the spiritual worlds depends greatly on the relationships they develop while working with the spirits there. Hence, it is a relationship-based activity that affects changes in the spiritual realms to foster healing of many types in the physical realm. In some areas, Shamanism is an active part of the dominant culture, and for others it directly contradicts the dominant culture. Some people's intuitions lead them to seek help from a shaman. For others, it is a last resort when they have run out of options; often, they don't even know anything about Shamanism.

Shamans have the ability to:

- Alter their state of consciousness at will and control themselves when entering and moving in and out of alternate states.
- Act as mediators between the needs of the physical world and the spirit worlds in ways understandable and useful to the community.
- Serve the needs of the people in ways that practitioners of other disciplines, such as priests, political leaders, psychiatrists, and physicians cannot.

Categories of healers

1. Traditional shamans
2. Shamans that bridge traditional shamanism and Western culture, often by adding rituals and ceremonies that don't necessarily come from their culture of origin.
3. Shamans called by the Divine to serve as shamans for the needs of the community, even if they were separated long ago from their original shamanic roots.

People seek shamans for healing many different ailments. If a person lives in a shamanic culture, going to a shaman for healing is usually part of a team approach, where the shaman partners up with nutritionists, physical healers, herbal practitioners, and other medical practitioners. In the Western world, shaman healing is usually rare. However, seeking contemporary shamans for health reasons is on the rise, especially for those who are not making progress with conventional approaches.

ANIMISM

First defined in 1871, animism is the concept that all things, inanimate and animate, possess an essence or spirit. Animism is a key component in many indigenous tribes' beliefs and ancient religions. It is the foundational characteristic of ancient spiritualism and is recognized in various forms throughout many modern religions worldwide. Animism is the concept that all things are connected by a spirit. These include people, objects, natural phenomena, animals, and geographic features. Today, animism is often used to discuss various systems of belief in anthropological terms.

Animists hold that all life is of spirit, not matter. Humans, animals, plants, rocks, mountains, and oceans all have souls. All are good or evil, but the relevant characteristic is not morality; it is power. Spirits or souls are living things with moods, volition, and the capacity to harm or to help. Those spirits that are not inhabiting a living thing exist in the form of angels, Goddesses, Gods, energy forces, and ghosts. To the animist, all events on earth have spiritual causes. Spirits influence either the disaster or the success of human beings. Many spirits can be vindictive or easily offended. Others can feel threatened and therefore have to defend themselves by causing harm to humans. When spirits are upset, they throw life off balance and cause all types of troubles, from hurricanes to headaches.

For these reasons, humans have shown deep respect to spirits throughout history through customs, rituals, and offerings. Pacifying spirits yields blessings and restores balance. If relationships with spirits are cultivated, they can be powerful allies against malicious beings. To animists, a community consists not only of the living, but also the unborn, a totem, and the deceased family members. A totem is usually a plant or animal that gains its lifesource from the same as humans within the same community.

Conception, birth, and death do not define the sentient state of a person, but are different states of a never-ending existence.

ALCHEMY

Alchemy is an ancient practice wrapped in secrecy and mystery. The practitioners of Alchemy were on a mission to manifest lead into gold, but their aspirations went far past merely creating some nuggets of gold. Their pursuits have excited the imagination of people for millennia! Alchemy was grounded in a spiritual and complex worldview. They thought that all things contain a spirit that is universal. Metals that grow in the earth were thought to be alive. When a common metal such as lead was discovered, it was believed to be an immature form of more significant metals like gold, both physically and spiritually. Alchemists believed that metals were not unique elements, but were substances in different developmental stages on a journey to spiritual perfection. While the science of alchemy was never proven, it did set the stage for modern chemistry.

CHURCH OF WICCA

The School and Church of Wicca was founded in 1968 by Yvonne and Gavin Frost. It was the first Wiccan church to be federally recognized in the United States. It is best known for its academic correspondence related to the unique interpretations of Wicca by the Frosts. The School and Church reside in Beckley, West Virginia (Grimassi, 2000). Thousands and thousands of students started the School of Wicca's 12-lesson course, but the course is rigorous and only a few thousand have completed it (Guiley, 2008). It is believed that the Church of Wicca is responsible for starting at least one hundred covens.

The Church of Wicca believes in monotheism; there is only one God. The founders of the Church hold the point of view that God is unknowable, abstract, and without need to be worshiped. This is the primary difference from other traditions of Wicca. Also, unlike most Wiccan covens, there is no focus on the feminine or female deities. The Frosts believed that there are idols and stone gods that humans create to store energy, which can then be used for magical workings. The Wiccan Church taught "Sidhe," the astral realm. It also taught that each individual's spirit travels through a reincarnation system where it can learn. They also believed that the world's overpopulation was due to "inferior spirits" taking human form on earth (Doyle, 2016).

The Church held instruction on the practice of kundalini sex, including "introitus," in which sexual activities without reaching a climax or orgasm were performed as an expression of surrender to God. The School of Wicca's curriculum offered a variety of classes about the Wiccan religion, metaphysical practices, and the occult. Interestingly, the first class is titled Essential Witchcraft, which takes "a year and a day" to complete. The school curriculum also contains courses on Psychic and Herbal Healing, Practical Sorcery, Astral Projection, Advanced Shamanism and Celtic Witchcraft, Prediction, Spiritual Awareness, Astrology, and many more topics.

FINDING THE RIGHT COVEN

Covens usually have up to 13 members, but are often smaller. Larger covens take a chance on finding it hard to keep the group dynamics healthy. There are no rules set in stone in Wicca, there is no one single guidebook, and no governing or ruling bodies. Each coven functions uniquely according to its members' and leaders' will. It is bound by an oath of secrecy, both to tradition and to members. Covens hold their meetings secretly in a location where they practice magic and rituals. How often they get together varies, but usually they do celebrate Sabbats (the Wheel of the Year) and Esbats (full moons).

It is essential for your journey that you find the right coven that is a good fit for you; no two are the same. Some practice Wicca with influence of different traditions, such as the faerie tradition or the northern tradition, so it is worth it to do your homework before asking to join a specific coven. It is kind of like buying a new car, don't jump on the first one you see. Seasoned groups usually tell you to shop around before committing to their membership.

Remember, Wicca is a religion that never proselytizes. They don't actively try to recruit new members. When joining a coven, you will most likely be asked to demonstrate a level of commitment. You should show that you are sure this is the only spiritual life you want to live. The initiation oath includes living a life of service and a willingness to make the craft a priority. Many Wiccans and pagans are secretive (still in the broom closet), so most covens don't advertise their locations or provide overt information. So, networking is important. You may want to start the "seeking" process, which means letting it be known you are looking to join a coven. After the word of you being a seeker spreads, you may be approached by a local coven.

There are also Wiccan and pagan websites for networking, such as Meetup groups or Witchvox.com, but make sure you practice normal online safety precautions, the same as you would when meeting any strangers. I always say, "Check it out." First, find, locate, and learn about your local Wiccan or pagan community. While it is not always obvious right off the bat, most areas have Pagan communities. Most pagan communities have a public facing aspect, as do Wiccan communities, so look for your tribe or coven providing classes or discussions (gatherings). Check out pagan book shops where they also generally have a noticeboard that lets you know the where and when of the local chapters. Once you go to some of the gatherings, you will begin to meet members of the Wiccan or pagan communities in a more social setting. Finding your coven is kind of like any other relationship. It is best done over time and gradually. Do not rush. Remember, this group includes people that you will be sharing your most vulnerable self with and the highs and the lows in your life. You want to be comfortable and feel safe sharing your secrets. They need to feel the same about you.

STEPS FOR STARTING A COVEN

1. Consider your main goals. How many members do you want in your coven? Do you know who your possible candidates are? What do you want to achieve? Will there be complete equality or a hierarchy? Sit down and journal all the questions you can come up with about your new coven, put them down for a week, and then go back and answer them.
2. Put together your coven's grimoire, after you have answered all of your questions. Seek out possible members for your coven and start planning your first get together.
3. Remember not to pressure anyone to join just because you are excited. They may wish to stay solitary witches or may already belong to an exclusive coven. Either way, respect their decision.
4. At your first gathering talk about the new ideas you have for the coven. Maybe you want some type of attire or uniform for your meetings and rituals? Maybe you want to collaborate with your new members on an apothecary. The possibilities are endless!
5. Don't push people too far. If someone doesn't want to do something or they feel uncomfortable, forcing them to do

something can give you a bad reputation. Give respect and you will receive it.
6. Due to the fact that society, still to this day, doesn't support Wicca (although things are starting to change), think about the importance of starting a secret coven.
7. Put together your materials, such as herbs, crystals, candles, and essential oils. Smudge bundles are always good to donate to a group. They are good to keep around in case someone forgets an item needed for spell casting or ritual work.
8. Make a coven calendar! Decide which Esbats and Sabbats you are going to celebrate as a coven. Write some rituals and spells together with your new coven members. Maybe you'll have a wonderful kitchen witch to whip up some blessed food for the celebration or have a potluck.
9. To help increase the power of your coven, study new types of magic and spiritual arts, so you and your coven can uncover even more mysteries. Find and read books of shadows and spell crafting books together. Dig deeper into learning your brand of magic. Avoid dogmatism and keep an open mind.

COVEN (THE WHEEL OF THE YEAR)

The Wheel of the Year is a religious celebration that occurs on each of the eight neo-pagan holidays. The Sabbats of the year include four festivals celebrating the changing seasons. The four solar festivals are: the fall equinox, summer solstice, spring equinox, and the winter solstice. The ancient Celts believed time was cyclical; people are born and die, seasons change, but all will again return in some aspect or another and the cycle repeats itself, naturally. Modern-day Wiccans celebrate the Wheel of the Year in remembrance of the importance of balance in an uncertain world. Jacob Grimm, an academic mythologist, coined the modern-day Wheel of the Year in 1835. By the 1950s it became solidified in the Wicca movement.

Wiccan Wheel of the Year Festivals

Name	Holiday	Earth Event	Date	Occasion
Samhain	Halloween	Scorpio	October 31st	Cleaning and releasing. Celebrating the dead.
Yule	Christmas	Winter Solstice Capricorn	December 20-25	Song, fellowship, candlelight, and lighting the sacred fire.
Imbolc	Candlemas	Midway between the Winter Solstice and the Spring Equinox: Aquarius	February 1-2	Lunar Fire Festivals, day of feast and celebration for the recovery of the Earth Goddess after giving birth.
Ostara	Easter	Spring Equinox Aries	March 20-23	Spring cleaning; planting seeds.
Beltane	May Day	Taurus	April 30-May 1	Fertility; Fire celebration. Couples dancing around the fire.
Litha	Midsummer	Summer Solstice Gemini	June 20-22	Gratitude for light and life. Honors the Sun God.
Lughnasadh	First Harvest	Halfway between the summer solstice and autumn equinox Leo	August 1	Symbolic gifts of the first fruits given to priests as an offering to deity. Honoring hard work and that pays off.
Mabon	Thanksgiving	Autumnal equinox Virgo	September 20-23	Time for resting after the hard work of the harvest. A time to reap what was sown. Time to finish up projects.

The eight Wiccan festivals are produced to bring awareness to all that has been gained or lost throughout the year. Ancient societies, such as the Celts, held the belief that a lack of gratitude was a sin that will take the sinner to a dark place, where bitterness, resentment, and self-pity live. In order to find balance in the world or in our lives, it is necessary to stop and reflect on those things we cherish and are grateful for.

SAMHAIN: HALLOWEEN

Samhain denotes the beginning of the yearly cycle. It marks the end of the season of light or summer and the start of the season of darkness. Darkness is not associated with negativity to those who are Wiccan. It doesn't mean evil or sadness, as there cannot be light without dark. It is merely part of the human condition. Thanks for the past year are put forth during the Samhain celebrations and Wiccans reflect on the wonderful times they share with those who recently passed on to the other side. Samhain celebration and rituals are very much like the modern-day Halloween festivities held in the United States. Samhain is a recognition of the "in-between" time, where the spirits of the dead can move into the realm of the living more easily. It is a Wiccan tradition to leave out snacks or to prepare a feast to leave out for those spirits visiting from the other realms.

Witches who in the past have done something wrong to someone who has passed over don't wear Halloween masks, so the spirits of those they have wronged will recognize them when they come back seeking requital. However, wearing a disguise or mask during Samhain is customary, in an effort to ward off those fairies, spirits, and dead souls with the strongest powers that move at night to seduce or abduct mortals. Mischievous activities, such as starting bonfires, are also traditional for Samhain. Pagans believe that the world started in chaos and that the Goddesses and other forces of the divine created balance and order. This is why Halloween pranks are done to represent this chaos. The returning to "normal" the following day symbolizes the restoration of order. Also, bonfires are lit to symbolize light amongst the darkness. This is a beautiful tradition.

YULE: CHRISTMAS

The winter solstice is celebrated as Yule when days start to become longer again. The winter solstice was seen by the ancient pagans as the birth of a new sun god of the year. Trees were traditionally believed to be sacred because they are home to deities and spirits. Very much like in Christmas traditions, an outdoor tree was decorated; in honor of the sun god's birthday, gifts were exchanged. Along with decorating a tree, bonfires were lit to symbolize the rebirth of light and new beginnings. People danced around the ignited Yule log, singing songs and tossing pieces of holly into the fire to represent the challenges of the past year. A piece of the Yule Log was kept for the next year's bonfire to symbolize continuity.

Also symbolized by Yule was the Oak King's victory over his brother, the Holly King. The entities of the two brothers represent the changing of the seasons. The earth is governed by the Oak King after his defeat of the Holly King in the winter, and he continues his reign until the coming of mid-summer or the Summer Solstice, when the Holly King retakes the battle, beating the Oak King. He then stays dominant during Yule. Wicca tradition is that the Oak King and the Holly King represent twin characteristics of the Horned God, with each one ruling half of the year. The battles are carried out to win the Goddess' favor, with the loser of the battle retreating to tend to his wounds for the other half of the year until he again returns to rule the Earth.

IMBOLC: CANDLEMAS

Imbolc takes place at the middle point between the Winter Solstice and the Spring Equinox, and corresponds with hope, pregnancy, purification, and fertility. In Old Irish, Imbolc means "in the belly of a pregnant sheep." The Imbolc festival represents a bright future, where dolls are weaved from wheat and corn stalks to pay tribute to Brigid, the Celtic goddess, and to symbolize continuity, good luck, and fertility. The fertility goddess, Brigid, is celebrated in early spring and marked in the United States by Groundhog Day.

OSTARA: EASTER

Ostara follows Imbolc and pays tribute to the Spring Equinox. Ostara celebrations mirror Easter festivities, including dying eggs, baby chicks, fancy feasts, and rabbits. The meaning of the word Ostara is rooted in the German lore as the fertility goddess and springtime. Eostre means mother of the dawn and in Wiccan tradition, she comes back from under the earth where she slept for the months leading up to her pregnancy with the next sun god to be born on each Yule.

Rebirth and renewal are emphasized on Ostara, which pays tribute to the importance of the egg symbolism. The notion of the labyrinth is also prominent. The labyrinth goes back to the Neolithic Age over 12,000 years ago, in areas as diverse as Ireland, India, and Greece. Ostara represents that aspect of yourself where you separate your personal external reality in search of a greater meaning unique to yourself. The traditional Easter Egg hunt is a portrayal of the search for heightened awareness.

BELTANE: MAY DAY

Beltane marks the coming of summer when bonfires burn freely in traditional Wiccan fashion. The bonfires of Beltane symbolize passion and the disinhibition of oneself to indulge in one's desires. The word "Beltane" means "bright fire" and represents fertility and light. Dancing is a common activity at a Beltane festival and circling a tree was common in ancient times. In modern days, people dance around a Maypole, which is a phallic symbol decorated with long strands of ribbon which are held by dancers as they circle around. Mayday is celebrated all over Europe and corresponds with Beltane. As dark days start to become increasingly light, all of nature awakens, including fairies, spirits, and other celestial entities. Pagans routinely enact cleansing rituals to protect themselves from mischievous fairy spells. They take lit candles to each corner of the home, from side to side and front to back, connecting eight points that set an invisible protective shield that manifests harmony and balance.

LITHA: MIDSUMMER/SUMMER SOLSTICE

Litha celebrates the longest day of the year, the Summer Solstice. The Holly King defeats his twin brother, the Oak King, on this day in June, and the days grow shorter. The festival of Litha is celebrated with a feast of honey cakes, fresh fruits, dancing, and bonfires. It is the commemoration of light overcoming the darkness with the knowledge that, in the future, the darkness will once again reign over the light. This signifies the temporary nature of longer nights and shorter days. Some people take marriage vows on Litha, as part of the festival. Sun wheels are constructed from wheat and corn stalks, and protection rituals are performed. Wiccans are very creative with their ritual plans on Litha. Water is blessed by magic to manifest abundance in their gardens and prosperity spells are cast under the night sky. Litha inspires inner power and brightness in all witches; small fires burn in the pots of one's home and the magic of love is in the air.

LUGHNASADH: FIRST HARVEST

Lughnasadh marks the change of season from summer to autumn, and it is celebrated with a harvest festival. The first fruits of the harvest are ceremoniously offered to the gods and goddesses. Lugh was the god of light in early Irish lore. His mother, Tailtiu, succumbed to the hard work of plowing and land preparation.

Lughnasadh is in honor of Lugh's mother's sacrifice; each year a funeral feast is held. Modern day pagan sport competitions include fencing, foot racing, horse-racing, and archery. It is also the last celebration before summer's end.

MABON: THANKSGIVING

Named in 1097, Mabon celebrates thoughts and Thanksgiving for all that has been gained and lost over the last year. It is the Autumn Equinox festival, named after the Welsh God, son of the Earth Mother Goddess, and symbolizes the second harvest. Wiccans and pagans alike bring seasonal gatherings, such as apples and grapes, and place them upon an altar, as they prepare a feast for family and friends. Apples are a common symbol of the second harvest and rituals give way in thanks to the gods and goddesses for the bountiful harvest of Mabon, as well as celebrating a day of equal light. On Mabon, night and day have an equal length. They are in perfect harmony once again. Feminine and masculine, light and dark, and inner and outer are perfectly balanced, but Mabon holds the cusp of change as the darkness begins to creep back upon the light of day. The days will grow shorter and begin to cool. The sap in the trees will return to their roots, and the green of the summer will again be transformed into wondrous oranges, golds, yellows, and the other fiery colors of fall, returning all to the darkness from whence we came.

Mabon is a time to give thanks for the Sun's diminishing light and for all the bounties provided. Each turn of the Wheel brings outer and inner gifts, insights, and a time for rest after the labor of the harvest. It is a time to finish our projects, clear out any clutter of what we no longer need or want, and prepare for the descent into winter. As we do this, we need to be looking forward to new hopes and aspirations and new ideas that will flourish in the dark, eagerly waiting for spring to return.

HERMETIC ORDER OF THE GOLDEN DAWN

The Hermetic Order of the Golden Dawn of the late 19th century was a magical order that practiced various types of spells and spiritualism. Magic and ritual concerts become the center stone of Wiccan and many other traditions. Much of today's spiritual magic was taken from the Golden Dawn tradition (Llewellyn Encyclopedia, 2008). Much like Masonic lodges, the Golden Dawn system was based on initiation and hierarchy. There are three Orders, with the "Golden Dawn" being the first; however, oftentimes, all three Orders are referred to as the "Golden Dawn."

The Golden Dawn Order provided teaching about the philosophy of the occult or esotericism, and was grounded in personal development and the Hermetic Qabalah through awareness and the study of the tarot, divination, astrology, geomancy, and the four classical elements. The Inner Order or the Second Order provided the teachings of magic, including astral projection, scrying, and alchemy; it was also called the Order of Rose of Ruby and Cross of Gold (Rosae Rubeae et Aureae Crucis). The Chiefs of Third Order of the Secret were said to be highly skilled spiritual communicators who directed the lower two order's activities.

CHOOSING A GOD OR GODDESS

To have a healthy relationship with a god or goddess, you need to establish a relationship. Like most relationships, you don't start one out of need, nor do you pick one out like you're choosing a handbag color. You do not have to believe in or worship a god or goddess to be a witch, and you don't have to pray to a specific god or goddess to be a pagan. However, it may be part of your spiritual practices to form some type of relationship with a named goddess or god but remember, in ancient history, most of the goddesses and gods were worshiped, and they usually had high priests who performed most of the work.

How to Choose a Matron or Patron Deity

In most pagan and witchcraft religions, "goddesses" and "gods" are frequently used terms. Some religions center their focus on gender duality, and some focus on just one god. You can believe in a single goddess or many, but Wiccan spend most of their time invested in Matron and Patron deities. You don't have to necessarily refer to them as Patron or Matron, some deities don't actually like the whole idea of being your Matron or Patron because they're not quite up to playing a parental role in your life. Some would much rather function as a well-respected peer or even Moon Goddess or Supreme Goddess. They are individualistic and they each desire something different from each one of us.

Most pagans worship some type of main deity or a few main deities, but it isn't necessarily a parental (fatherly or motherly) type of a relationship. The exact type of relationship you will have with your deities depends on both you and the deity involved. No two people worship the same way. You can start with books and the internet. When you find a spirit whose qualities you like, give them some time and a few offerings over a period of a month or so. Ask them for a sign that they hear you. You may receive an animal sighting, a recurring number, a song, or you may feel their impact directly on some area of your life that suddenly improves. Once contact is established, invoke them in your spell crafting, starting with something small, or send them a prayer. Always remain sure that your initial requests sit firmly in the deity's wheelhouse. Journal your results. Did you enjoy their energy? Was your request fulfilled? If your results were positive, continue to offer thanks and provide offerings, always asking for signs and opening your mind to seeing them.

You can target a deity based upon your life circumstances, local spirits, or a specific deity you would like to honor. You can use a search engine to come up with links, books, and pages about every specific deity from any specific pantheon. Look into the Elements and Spirits, Gods and Goddesses of healing, justice, culinary works, or anything else. However, these should just be jumping off points to your in-depth research.

Other types of documents:

- Legends and myths
- Archaeological and historical evidence and books.
- Poems and hymns
- Texts written by individuals involved in reconstructionism.

WORSHIPPING AND WORKING WITH A DEITY

Not all goddesses and gods are the same, so it's essential to your spiritual life to get to know the ones you want to work with. The idea of the appropriate or right way to worship and give offerings should be in a way that is conducive to the needs or demands of the goddess or god in question. Get to know the legends and myths related to the respected group they are associated with and study these stories. For instance, if you are devoted to the Greek goddesses and gods, read Homer's writings and hymns. If your path is Celtic, go over the *Mabinogion*, and reach out and ask them to flat-out tell you what they need.

Put some thoughts into how you honor the Goddesses and Gods. Ask yourself what you want to achieve by making the offering. Maybe you are just expressing your gratitude or maybe you have a specific request. The most important thing to do when trying to worship or work with a deity is to study those divine beings of your tradition, so that when you conduct a ritual in their name or give an offering, you can do it in a way that truly honors them.

2

HOW TO LEARN MAGIC IN THE MODERN WORLD

MAGIC IS USED EVERY DAY BY MILLIONS IN THE MODERN WORLD, whether you believe it or not! Modern day society puts great effort into controlling people's perceptions and thoughts about the everyday world. Agenda setting theory is a social engineering technique that aims to vastly shift our perception and used to be called psychological warfare. Magic is a way to take your power back and control the events in your life, rather than being a victim of mass media's brainwashing.

WHAT IS MAGIC AND HOW IT CAN HELP YOU?

Magic is a personal journey in which you learn how to use your senses to navigate this world. Modern magic is often defined as accomplishing the impossible. The accepted definition of magic is utilizing perception to interact with and influence the world. We shouldn't think of it as "doing the impossible" because that pushes magic into fantasy rather than a method for improving the quality of our lives. Over the last thousand years, religion and science have shoved magic to the outer edges of perception and essentially taken it out of the hands of people. Science and religion seem to have claimed the exclusive right to shape how people perceive the world. Nowadays, society leaves people with little choice about what faith is and then punishes those who have the courage to look at the world differently. Because of this, society's development is skewed. The world needs magic. We need to have the ability to perceive all of the options life has to offer and allow us to function as explorers in life.

For many individuals, magic is just another way of connecting with your potential. You use your perception and intuition to explore your available potential and then pick an action to tap into that potential. It isn't uniquely special as some may think, as is the case when any real-life event gets compared to movies. Working with your potential is a way to help you connect to what is hidden to your normal senses and what is in plain sight. Part of magic is learning how to carefully listen to the silence.

COLLECTING MAGICAL ENERGY

There are many different types of magical energy. Let's divide it into three magical categories: spiritual, mental, and physical. Most people's perceptions revolve around the physical world, so this is where the average person sees magic. There are also many magic styles:

1. Transformation or alteration: Rearranging the definition of something.
2. Evocation or conjuration: Becoming aware of something new.
3. Divination: Gathering new information and exploring new insights.

Spirits are real, but they don't directly manifest into the physical world. Just because something is real, doesn't make it a physical reality. Society is a real entity but not a physical one, it exists only in our minds. Society is a manifestation of people who then construct physical artifacts. Certain physical manifestations of society act as reinforcements for a society that is consumer-based.

Spirits are representations of reality; they are not of the physical world. When we experience something spiritual, it is a description of an experience which is outside of the physical. After the spiritual experience is complete, the individual is left with a memory which is then understood as a mind-based experience. Unfortunately, the media and wishful thinking encourages us to magnify our spiritual experiences, much like those tales told about the size of the fish you caught that expand over time. So, spiritual magic is very real, but tends to be much more subtle that one might think and not nearly as flashy.

We are a microcosm and a macrocosm; we are each an individual, while at the same time, we are the universe. Magic based in the spiritual realm is subtle. Since spirit is independent of the physical world, using spirit (real magic) is much like constructing a sandcastle, a temporary structure. It is not attempting to attach itself to reality, yet it does impact the world and then it gently washes away. As you continue to see and learn magic, remember it is subtle, not long lasting. But what is everlasting? Even the vastness of the mountains, with time, erodes to sand. Just as a firefly will only dance for an evening, the magical experience can only last in the form of a story.

MAGIC AND MODERNITY

As the exploration of spirituality outside of the boundaries of traditional religion continues to grow, ritual and spell crafting and magical ways of healing are now attracting the interest of the masses. What is quickly becoming an acceptable form of spiritualism was once banished to the outer fringes of society. Meditation, tarot, and astrology and other beginner-level concepts have given way to an interest in astral projection, aura cleansing, reiki, spellcrafting, moon worshipping, and dream reading for many people.

Modern life can be very chaotic and it's perfectly crafted to take us away from being present. Rituals are a practice in mindfulness. Tea ceremonies and meditation are ancient methods of grounding. People are looking for a more spiritual and sacred way of life. We are all seeking a deep connection with other people, plants and animals, the elements, and ourselves. We want to be one with nature again, rather than sticking out like a sore thumb. We need that balance in order to help us during these trying times.

BRINGING TECHNOLOGY INTO MAGIC

Advanced, ever-present magic almost always seems to work the same as technology. Car engines are powered by the element fire, but we don't think about it like that, we just get in them and drive away. We don't need to acquire special talents to use our phones, as they appear to work like magic. There's even a new word, "magitech," a combination of modern technology and magic. Magic and technology have science in common, in that they are things to be learned, studied, and experimented with.

Living in this modern digital age can have serious mental health consequences. Social media and the ability of others to reach us 24/7 provide people with more opportunities to access our auric fields and our energy supply. Don't worry though, magic comes to the rescue. We can use your magical tools for protection in the technological realm, just like we do for protection in other realms. It is like having a protection spell for your phone.

Enacting magic that impacts the technological realm, or technomancy, improves the way machines work, can elevate our status on social media, and can help to ward off negative confrontations with others online (Stardust, 2021). We should perform technomancy at least every other day. Here are some tips on how to perform technomancy:

1. Smudge your phone with *palo santo* or *sage* to release static energy. Our cell phones are like a gateway to the world. This is why it is so important to cleanse the energy we receive and give. This can help to make sure we are receiving positive and constructive information, not the type that causes distress or blurs our judgement.
2. Keep a *shungite* or *black tourmaline* crystal near your phone. Shungite is a healing and purifying stone, so it is perfect for mending anyone you may have argued with. It also helps you dissociate your energy from those psychic leeches who won't stop calling you. Black tourmaline cleanses our devices and removes unwanted or negative energy. Crystals are excellent detoxifying agents and will help you to gain better privacy, while at the same time boosting your likes on social media because they draw positive energy and people are drawn to positivity.
3. Envision sacred geometry. Picturing sigils or pentagrams or other powerful symbols project divine protection. Just like in other areas of life, projection magic makes sure we don't receive hateful drama in our electromagnetic realm, and only allows positive energies to enter into our smart devices.
4. Keep your mantras close by. Have a mantra on hand to help you if you find yourself arguing, gossiping, or experiencing any other type of negativity in a conversation. "Delete, cancel, block, clear" is one affirmation that will bounce gloomy sentiments off of your auric field, so it doesn't influence your positive vibrations.
5. Keep your mindset golden. Imagine a golden glow around

your computer or phone. It will ward off haters and pull in more positive people.

FINDING YOUR MAGIC PLACE

It seems obvious to trust your intuition; however, like everything in life, refining your intuition takes practice and skill. Throughout the day, we are confronted with pressure, suggestions, and opinions from the outside world; what is right and what is wrong, and what we shouldn't or should do. During our development, the challenges we face are supposed to build our confidence and self-esteem; however, that doesn't always happen and instead we stuff our inner voice deep within us to accept someone else's views. To find your way, you need to know who you are, you have to know your beliefs, and what makes you happy and what makes you sad. Learning how to use your intuition or your inner compass can help you do those things. When you're faced with a problem or a choice, the first place you should seek an answer is within, so the advice you get is from someone you can trust.

First, you should be learning how your intuition works. Is it a slight grumbling in the back of your mind or a word or image in your head? A feeling you should turn right instead of left? Acquiring the skill of identifying how your intuition presents itself and the difference from feeling like a passing thought will help you to practice ways in which you can pay attention to how and when your intuition manifests. It can also present itself in shadow work, in your dreams, via tarot, or during a nature walk.

Witches have learned how to finely tune their intuition, but newer witches have to learn how to trust it. One way to learn how to listen to your intuition is to stop thoughts that try to interfere with it. For instance, you are on a shopping trip and you suddenly get a thought that you left the oven on. Immediately afterward you get another thought that discredits your intuition and tells you that you worry too much. There are many ways we have been conditioned to not pay attention to our intuition. Pay attention to yourself, don't ignore that voice. Listen to learn and learn to listen! Maybe you get an uneasy feeling about traveling on some road that you normally take or an uneasy feeling about purchasing something online. It is not really about if it comes true, it is about taking every opportunity to practice listening and learning how to decipher what your intuition is trying to tell you through experimentation. As you learn and practice listening to yourself, your intuition will become stronger, and you will be able to rely on it more. Try wearing pearls or moonstone crystals to sharpen your intuition and learn how to listen.

FRANK'S BOOST YOUR INTUITION SPELL

Materials:

- Pearl or moonstone crystal
- Silver coin
- Clear quartz crystal
- Rosemary
- Lemongrass oil
- A blue candle

Instructions

1. Smudge the area and sit in a comfortable position.
2. Anoint your blue candle with the lemongrass oil.
3. Light the candle.
4. Place the moonstone or pearl crystal in one hand and the clear quartz in the other hand and place your hands in your lap.
5. Place the coin between you and the candle, creating a symbolic bridge of elements from the flame to your body.

6. Close your eyes, center yourself, and chant:

> *Grant me the intuition: That I may know my truth*
> *With moonstone in my hand*
> *And pearls of wisdom from the sand*
> *Let chaos be gone*
> *With the silver of the dawn*
> *Make me bright like the snow: From within I will know*
> *So mote it be*

DAILY PASSIVE MAGIC

Meditation is one of the daily passive magical practices of Wicca. In order to manifest effective magic, you need to acquire the skill of entering a place within you that is calm and deeply relaxed in order to align and balance yourself with the natural energies and forces around you. As you learn to be still and quiet your mind and enter into a deep state of calmness, you will learn how to become centered, focused, and balanced; you are learning how to mentally discipline yourself. It is in this place in your inner being that you will join together with your spirit self and your guide through the path you have chosen to take. You can use your magical tools to help you on your journey, such as candles, incense, music, singing, chanting, drumming, and guided imagery to put your mind into a meditative state.

Once you learn how to listen to your spirit and trust yourself, options begin to appear. Things that seemed vague or impossibly subtle begin to become clear and attainable in your awareness because you have a better understanding of yourself. You can visualize your near future and the choices you are about to make that may be wrong or right. Many things will come to you while in this state that projects you into the space between the material and celestial.

Another daily passive magical activity is a simple walk in the park or somewhere in nature. It has the astonishing power to enhance your well-being, realign your spiritual awareness, and broaden your knowledge as a witch. Wildcrafting is one way to get in touch with your daily magical practices. Instead of buying a $55 wreath from Walmart or a craft shop, take a walk, find some beautiful evergreens, and create something wonderful with the magic of a tree. Take a course on wild edibles and then look for a few while on your walk. Cooking with lavender, wild onions, and wild berries puts the magic of plants right in your tummy. Check out the tiniest details while on your magical nature walk. Look at the tiny flowers, and the veins running through the leaves, and the penny-sized mushrooms you came close to stepping on. These are magical things. The geometric magic of a honeycomb and the sweeping, broad landscapes will leave you with a wild sense of wonder.

There are endless ways to practice daily passive magic; even when it comes to your evening showers, there is magic to be had. Spiritual bathing has more intent than just cleaning off and it has been used traditionally in every culture, often to cleanse the soul, heal your chakras, and heal your spirit. Spiritual bathing clears blockages that can often lead to more serious problems. You have to make your tub a sacred space. That means no clutter and a spic-n-span tub. You add the magic in the form of oils, herbs, flowers, and most of all intention. You need to focus on spiritual healing, so that means unplugging all of your smart devices.

SPEAKING TO THE NATURE OF SPELLS

Nature plays a huge role in the Wiccan culture and magic. One of the ways we speak to the nature of spells is by physically connecting with the elements, starting with the earth. Earthing is the spiritual process of experiencing magic by physically connecting with the earth. Touching the earth brings together the spiritual and the physical. Studies have indicated that skin to earth contact has a significant effect on our wellness, both physically and emotionally (Oschman et al., 2015). The body's stress hormones are reduced, blood pressure is lowered, heart rate decreases, and an overall calming effect results from earthing or skin-to-earth contact (Chevalier et al., 2019). Connecting to the earth this way may also introduce you to the local spirits wishing to start a relationship with you!

Many pagans, Wiccans, pantheists, and New Agers practice nature religion, the oldest magic spell of them all. As previously discussed, variants of animism and a belief in the forces of nature, as well as a belief in the spiritual realms, are common themes to most nature religions. Even those adhering to scientism and atheism, who hold the belief that nature does not hold magic, still accept the fact that it has the ability to generate feelings of wonder, mystery, and awe, all of which are mystical. Many Wiccans and pagans are focused on green magic and the concept that deities and other powers of the supernatural realms can be recognized through directly experiencing natural objects and natural events. Monotheism is part nature religion and many people believe that nature as one entity is sacred and even divine. There are no scriptures, prophets, and holy books in this religion. However, it does serve society through focusing on our connection with nature.

In the spirit of the nature religion, all things of the universe (not created by humans) are collective and bonded by a labyrinthine web of life force or energy, including humans. All members are considered clergy, with both women and men found in leadership positions for ritual events, but only temporarily. There are no permanent hierarchical relationships established in nature religion. There are no buildings erected for gatherings. Sacred spaces for ritual are in the natural environment, not in brick-and-mortar establishments. This is not to say that members of nature religions do not have get-togethers in someone's home, because gatherings to plan religious activities in nature can be structured in such a way.

CONTROLLING YOUR ENERGY

Energy is a tangible, moving life force that is easily understandable in the context of our day-to-day feelings (lethargic and sluggish or the opposite, invincible). Usually we blame our days of low energy on unhealthy food or a lack of a good night's sleep. It is, however, much more complex than that. We can have a conscious relationship with our energy system. Sometimes, we really complicate the concept of energy by trying to define it in mystical or scientific terms. To really understand what it is, all you have to do is be still and feel into your surroundings and yourself. For instance, when we are crying or laughing, we may feel a release of energy. When feeling calm, we're grounded.

Certain people or circumstances can drain our energy. Also, sometimes when we are in situations in life where we feel less than ideal, we may lean on others using their energy as our own fuel source. Even our personal boundaries are a source of energy. We can let our energy openly flow when we want to share with others, or tighten it up when we want to detach. One of the things we learned in elementary science class is that energy cannot be destroyed but it can be altered. When depleted of energy, a system can collapse. Despite the strength of its power, energy on its own is neutral. It is our consciousness that decides its direction and movement. If we comprehend what it means to be conscious of our energy, we can better direct our energy toward connection, evolution, and creation. The less we comprehend how to be conscious of our energy, the more stagnant, separated, and even self-destructive we become.

I learned a great deal about how to restore my energetic integrity and what it means for my energy systems to be blocked. All of us know what it feels like to be open and flexible. When our energy is flowing freely, we breathe easier and have an overall sense of spaciousness. When our energy flow is balanced, our mind, body, and spirit work with each other in partnership. We trust ourselves and the process. This is called energetic integrity. Many of us feel that energetic integrity is temporary. Sometimes, it seems blocked, stuck, or stagnant. Our thinking becomes narrower and more fixed. We breathe unevenly, sometimes holding our breath, and feel our muscles begin to tighten or weaken. There is a general feeling of being ungrounded or detached from our power. Sometimes, it feels like we lose our footing, which is a feeling of being unbalanced and only able to act submissively or aggressively.

We often tend to block out our personal energy to avoid unwanted impulses or feelings. Very similar to repressing our emotions, this is a defense mechanism that allows us to block unwanted thoughts or emotions. For instance, think about a school-age child. Every day, the child goes to school and runs up to her teacher proudly handing in her homework on time. Each time she does this, her teacher places the homework in a pile, and instructs the child to take her seat. The child senses this as a form of rejection, and begins to restrict her feelings of excitement and her impulse to run up to her teacher. She starts to tell herself a story so she can make sense of her experience. Over time, repressing her emotions will begin to contract her energy flow. When the little girl grows up, we may see an adult who struggles with expressing her feelings and may have physically distant relationships. Her life may have the main goal of avoiding humiliation and rejection and the associated pain that accompanies it at all costs.

It takes a bit of self-exploration to learn how to restore your energetic integrity. It takes willingness, patience, and risk. It becomes a task of learning how to become increasingly conscious of your energy flow and to learn how to use your energy to stay separate or to defend. It is about getting in touch with your belief systems and notice where you distort reality as a means of adapting. With time, you can start to see the different methods you use your energy to defend yourself against certain emotions and experiences. Only then can you appreciate how manipulating your energy in this way blocks you from reaching your full potential that comes with embracing your energy as a full life force.

At first, I thought this was an avenue for personal growth, then I began to understand the relationship between my consciousness and my own energy. That translated into understanding the connection between consciousness and energy in systems as a whole within which we live. This applies to politics, our family life, the way we interact with the environment, finances, and even war. For instance, what if monetary wealth is just a cognitive distortion regarding safety? When we lack the consciousness of our energy flow, distortions can be found just about everywhere in ourselves and in society. If we start the work of transforming distorted energy back into its natural flow, we will be able to effect actual change in both society and in ourselves.

Steps for how to get to know you own energy system:

1. Thoughts are energy forms, so start to generate an awareness of your thinking. Start with the first thought you have upon waking and take it from there. Notice how and when your thoughts are flexible (how things can be) or fixed (how they are).
2. Several times per day, pause and close your eyes. Travel inward and check on if you feel present, how you are breathing, if you are relaxed or tense, tired or rested.
3. Take the time to move different parts of your body and notice if any feelings or thoughts arise. Are there some parts of your body that create emotions when energized by movement? Roll your head across your shoulders and note your feelings.

4. Make vocal sounds, either alone or with other people. Energize your "no" and "yes." Is one easier to say than the other? Are you even willing to make a sound?
5. Ask yourself where the energy currents are in your life. Are you emotionally fatigued by the demands of others or are you forcing your energy onto other people or situations?
6. Notice the changes in your energy levels when in the presence of different people. Does your breathing change? Do your muscles contract?
7. Get together with a friend and play around with your energetic boundaries. Stand in front of each other and slowly walk towards each other and check out when you start to feel their energy. Does their energy make you feel less grounded? Can you use your voice to ask them to back away or to come closer? Feel the energy.
8. Journal your feelings according to your beliefs, and write down where in your body you feel these feelings if you feel them at all.
9. How do you approach the world? Do you lead with your hands, heart, or head?
10. Ask other people how they experience your energy.

MODERN MAGICAL ENERGY

Modern magic, like all things in life, can't operate without fuel. How far can you travel in your car without stopping for gas? How long can you go without a meal? Everything in the universe needs nourishment, including your spirit. Increasing your supply of energy to fuel your magic is a powerful way to enhance your spell work. If you want to practice real magic, you need real power, the type that doesn't run out and leave you spiritually stranded. There are many forms of modern magic activities you can use to raise your energy levels, such as dancing, chanting, drumming, forest bathing, and even sex. These are all powerful ways for enhancing your magical powers, but the real witch crafting comes from learning how to harness the power of the universe to manifest your desires, your destiny, and your sacred self. It takes a richer, deeper, and wider approach to energy work, one that moves you past your limitations and into spiritual enlightenment. Lifting up energy and projecting it to manifest your intent, is the modern way of working with energy to make magic or cast a spell. It is what happens when you learn how to really use your wand.

Remember, the universe is half feminine and half masculine and they both need each other for fertile and generative life processes to exist. The courtship and joining of the feminine and masculine are the energy that transforms, moves, and creates the universe. Likewise, while projecting energy is a powerful source of magic, the ability to receive it is just as powerful a tool. The following are six types of modern magical energy:

1. *Arcane Energy*: Glowing light is the most magical type of energy with an unknown origin. It is the energy of black magic, found within spell books and magical items that bend the very fabric of reality to manifest intent and desire.
2. *Death Energy:* The energy produced from decay and death is naturally forming. Its color is dark purple, black, or putrid green and it occurs naturally in crypts, tombs, and things that have decayed for a very long time. This type of energy is used like grasping hands to drain its victims of their energy level.
3. *Aesthete Energy:* This corresponds with all things beautiful, such as aurora borealis, clouds, and vistas. This energy field forms around beautiful objects in nature or natural works of art. It can be manifested by those with artistic skills in music and poetry. This energy is not seen, yet travels like music and enhances everything it touches. Magic songs

created by elves and fairies can lure people into a trance, or can be used to enchant a place or person with beauty.

4. *Glacial Energy:* This energy pertains to glaciers and ice and the unfeeling and unchanging cold. It can be found in icicles, glaciers, and other ancient frozen zones or it can even be the downy fur plucked from a newborn penguin.
5. *Verdant Energy:* This energy is the energy of nature and its color is bright green or dark red. It is a powerful energy that is overpowering and uncontrolled and is only found in the bellows of the most massive and ancient of trees. When conquered by a witch, it doesn't just make them more powerful or heal them, it also sharpens their senses to become equal to those of an animal. This type of energy is hardly ever used, except by Druids; even they are very careful and keep it at the end of a long wand or stick to avoid being contaminated.
6. *Interspatial Energy:* This energy is hidden in spaces within other spaces. It can be harvested carefully from complex architectures. Its color is clear or a dark orange glow. It gathers underneath things and in corners. When used as magic, it holds the keys to the realms within or interspatial realms. These realms are filled with symbols, creatures, and treasures of the inner spaces. When used carefully, it can unleash your hidden potential or even lessen the weight of one's soul.

3

DIFFERENT TYPES OF WITCHCRAFT AND WITCHES

THERE ARE VARIOUS TYPES OF WITCHES IN THE WORLD TODAY. FOR most witches, spell casting and magic are considered a skill set, and not always a form of religion. Therefore, people of any religion can practice magic no matter what their spiritual background is. There are also many types of witchcraft that are well-suited for all areas of our lives.

MODERN WITCHCRAFT

The meaning of modern witchcraft depends on who you ask. To most of us, a witch is the epitome of owning your own truth and all the power that comes with it. To wiccans, witches are religiously affiliated with the beliefs and traditions of Wicca. To some other witches, magic is part of their wellness regime or a manifestation of their creativity. Most modern witchcraft entails altar assemblies, spell work, and rituals. Modern witchcraft affords witches the opportunity to attend a fall-equinox ritual or sign up for magic-making classes. The use of candles, crystals, essential oils, and herbs in magic has become a very lucrative industry. Witches can be sought online to purchase spells made to fit your needs, and some witches are hired to cast spells on your behalf.

GENETIC WITCHCRAFT

As you come to know more individuals involved in paganism, you will sometimes come across someone who claims to be a genetic witch or that they were born a witch. However, there is no such thing as "witch DNA." But there isn't any Christian, Hindu, or Muslim DNA either. Being Wiccan usually means believing and doing things in such a way that makes you a witch. However, you can be raised in a Wiccan family, but that doesn't make you a "born Wiccan."

Some people are born with greater psychic abilities than others and they may run in their family, but as far as identifying witch chromosomes, there is no such thing. However, I believe we all have psychic abilities and we just have to learn how to tap into them, rather than repressing them, as most people do. Oh, and by the way, people with Salem ancestry are not witches either. But certainly, there are hereditary witchcraft traditions; however, they are not inherited genetically. Some witchcraft traditions are passed down through generations and they tend to keep strong ties with the family of origin's witchcraft practices. For instance, some families follow Celtic gods, and practice a tradition of folk magic.

KITCHEN WITCHCRAFT

Using magic when preparing food for loved ones is like adding some tender love and care (TLC) to each dish. TLC is the strongest magical ingredient used in kitchen witchcraft. Preparing meals with your own two hands and herbs from your windowsill infuses your dishes with magic. There is a sacredness in kitchen witchcraft that can change the way you imagine, prepare, and enjoy your meals. Kitchen witchcraft is spell work at its most basic level. The more you develop your magical repertoire, the more you will realize the wealth of magic that can be performed on a daily basis.

Kitchen witchcraft involves some wonderful magical tools, cauldrons, and candles. A stovetop altar creates an ambiance that is magically inspired. Keeping the kitchen as a sacred space is a very important component to kitchen witchery. There is no harmony in chaos and clutter. A Book of Shadows just for your kitchen will keep a tally of your culinary witchcraft. Chanting while stirring, in either deosil (clockwise) or widdershins (counterclockwise) direction is like adding fairy dust to your recipe.

HUMANITIES WITCHCRAFT

There are federally recognized and well-respected Wiccan nonprofit religious groups today. Their covens charge no dues or tithes. While Christian, Muslim, and Jewish churches qualify for grant monies to the tune of millions, pagans and Wiccans do not. However, humanitarian witchcraft does participate in the following activities:

- Activism: Spiritual and social programs, medical marijuana, peace, and others.
- Advocacy: On behalf of persecuted and abused pagans.
- Divination: Global efforts and hundreds of methods of divination.
- Education: Clergy training, interviews, lectures, mentions (in numerous books), tours, writing articles, books, and websites.
- Herbal: Resources, aid, guidance.
- Home: Acquisition, blessing, ghost-banishing, selling.
- Inmates: Nationwide Pagan advocacy.

- Legal: Aid, child custody cases, resources, unfair laws, and policies elimination.
- Magical: Aid, guidance, teaching.
- Medical: Aid, guidance, resources.
- Military: Conscientious objector and base coven advocacy.
- Personal: Counseling.
- Rites: All rites of passage, elaborate/free public Sabbats, handfasting, legal marriages, rites for departed souls.

CRIMINAL WITCHCRAFT

Most have learned about the infamous Salem witchcraft trials, but there were many more. In some regions of the world, there are still laws prohibiting the practice of witchcraft. In the U.S. there are laws in some states making divinatory practices and fortune telling a criminal offense, to protect vulnerable citizens from the many swindles of con artists. Wiccans and pagans, alike, need to be familiar with their rights as an employee, parent, or active force military personnel. However, these are more along the lines of anti-fraud laws, not anti-witchcraft, and are usually part of zoning regulations.

There are reported cases in the U.S. in which certain witchcraft practices have been taken to court. This happened mostly in cases of animal sacrifice rituals that were deemed a public health concern and a violation of animal cruelty acts. Specifically, in New Orleans, this law burdens the free exercise of religious practices. However, one case was overturned because there was not sufficient evidence in support of the health concern and the courts ruled in favor of the right to practice animal sacrifice. This is a hot topic for pagans and Wiccans, with valid arguments on both sides.

Wiccans and other earth-based practitioners have equal rights with all other citizens of this country. Like everyone else, your legal rights against religious discrimination apply. Make sure you document each and every event if you are a victim of discrimination. Remember, if it's not documented, it didn't happen. Journal any events or conversations as they happen in real time. It is important to understand that opinions and discrimination are two different things. You are being religiously discriminated against if you are denied unalienable rights on the basis of your religion.

Your rights as a Wiccan or pagan parent stand when your child attends a United States public school, the same as any other parents' rights. Keep in mind that most teachers have not had Wiccan or pagan students in their classroom before. With that said, here is an opportunity for setting a precedent for other pagan and Wiccan students. If your child comes home and tells you that their teacher said something unkind, don't rush off to the school board, go and talk to the teacher.

Let's say you have decided to come out of the "broom closet" and you are facing getting fired from your job because of it, even though you have an excellent work history. In this case, you should seek the advice of a civil rights lawyer who specializes in Wiccan and pagan discrimination cases. Remember to document every event.

If you or someone you care about are a member of the military, familiarize yourself with your rights as a Wiccan or pagan soldier. First, go through the proper military channels, if you or a person you know suffers religious discrimination. If that doesn't work, contact the Inspector General (IG). They shoulder the responsibility for investigating these types of complaints. If you still do not experience positive results, you can file an Article 138 complaint (Wigington, 2020).

GRANDMOTHERLY WITCHCRAFT

Many of us come from a long line of witches. Sometimes this knowledge is kept hidden until a child comes of age and can make their own decisions regarding witchcraft. But, if you are wondering if you come from a lineage of witches, here are ten telltale signs that your grandmother(s) may have been witches:

- *Elixirs and Potions*: Grandmotherly witchcraft usually has a potion for just about everything. It is the first turn-to when you feel under the weather. They can taste awful, but they do the trick.
- Castor oil is well known for its healing properties, and is referred to as "palm of Christ" or "Palma Christi" in some cultures.
- Cinnamon
- Garlic
- Onion
- Honey
- Lemon
- Salt
- Corked-topped glass bottles containing tinctures.
- Pot liquor: the liquid leftover after making greens (kale or collard greens) and used as a tincture.
- Wheat germ
- Goldenseal
- Weeds and roots pulled from the backyard
- *Spirits:* Grandmotherly witchcraft is always chock full of spirits: nefarious spirits, friendly spirits, old spirits, and even spirits cloaked in black. Grandmothers do not seem particularly worried and are usually accustomed to the spirits they live with, as well as the occasional visitors. They are rarely evil spirits; they just are who they are!
- *Unflinching Grandmothers*: There is little that rattles or

shakes grandmothers. This is just part of the natural outcome of them knowing who they are and their powers. The grandma of one of my friends was sitting at a baseball game when a drunk spectator started falling down the bleachers right toward her. She didn't bat an eye. Suddenly, two teenage boys jumped in front of her and broke the man's fall. Not a hair on her body was touched. She never flinched.

- *Hair:* Grandmotherly witches do not have bad hair days. Every once in a while, a strand may jump right at you. Their hairbrushes are laced with magic, and the hair caught in their brushes is then used in spell work. They always seem to have a lot of hair, too.
- *Ageless*: Grandmother witches don't age like "normal" people. It is very difficult to tell their age, as if they have always existed in a time warp. I am sure they know how to tinker with time because I find myself warping it, too.
- *The Color Purple*: Grandmotherly witchcraft is full of purple and includes purple clothes, purple candles, purple crystals, purple plants, purple potions, etc. It is no surprise that purple is the color of royalty as well. It has the highest vibration of all of the colors, so you will often see grandmother witches only writing in purple ink. My friend's grandmother, who is a witch, has a purple front door!
- *Old Wive's Tales*: "Wait fifteen minutes after you eat before you go swimming." "Red sky at night, sailor's delight, red sky in morning, sailor's warning." Grandmotherly witchcraft is the origin of many old wives' tales, which often turn out to be true.
- *Baby and Birthing Rituals*: Some of the witchcraft rituals I know about are lightly tapping a silver coin on a baby's belly button, whispering a protection spell in the baby's ear, and walking the baby's house perimeter while singing. The

miracle of birth mirrors magic in so many ways, which is part of the reason midwives and witches have a connection. Grandmotherly witchcraft lore states that if a pregnant woman has heartburn, the baby will have a full head of hair. And being born "under a veil or caul" means that you have psychic powers.

- *Psychic Powers Full of Predictive Abilities.* Witchy grandmothers can feel in their bones what the weather will be like the following day, they answer the phone before it rings, and almost always know the direction a relationship is headed. You will often hear grandmother witches saying, "It is as good as done!"
- *Viscerally Connected to Nature:* The old witch living in the forest can tell you everything there is to know about celestial life. Plant and herb magic, the magic of berries, and long conversations with elves, gnomes, and fairies are just part of the everyday life of grandmotherly witches.

ETHNIC WITCHCRAFT

Black American witchcraft has its origins in West Africa, where Yoruba was born. Yoruba is a set of religious lore centered on recognition for ancestors and worship of orishas (a diverse group of deities). Those West African traditions came to America with slavery, and eventually combined with Catholicism, and other Western religions. By the 1800s, voodoo, hoodoo, and other fusions descended from West African religions. Most ethnic witches from this background practice with incense, water, and candles. Such minimal tools became a great source of power because the witches didn't have access to much more. Modern day African American witches have added a millennial touch to their Yoruba-based religions. Altars are erected to honor ancestors so they can ask their advice on everything from career advancement to relationships. Casting banishment spells with emoji magic to treat depressions, sage rituals, and crystal work are just a few of the modern black witchy ways.

Caribbean and Latin American witchcraft cultures have vast spiritual and religious practices. Two of these are the foundation of Latin American witchcraft known today as healing magic (santiguos) and spiritual cleansing (despojos), which are the underlying powers beneath divination, amulets, spells, offerings, and concoctions (brebajes). Haitian Vodou, Brujería, Umbanda, and Brazilian Candomblé are just of the few modern-day religions of Latin witchcraft. Constructing sacred altars and the use of white, red, and black magic to summon ancient spirits and demons, elements of nature for healing, love, beauty, and prosperity are some of the magical practices of the contemporary Latino Witch. Latino witchcraft practitioners provide popular online services as sorcerers that can repair damages caused by jealousy, unfaithfulness, and humiliation. The amount of Latin and Caribbean witchcraft practices is higher in Canada and the U.S. than in other countries.

Asian witchcraft is heavily influenced by Taoism and shamanistic divination. Chinese American witches can feel a certain disconnect from the resources available to them. Asian witchcraft doesn't really identify only with tarot decks, dedication altars, Aleister Crowley studies, and herbs and oils. Western occultism can offer Asian witches peace of mind, but they really would like to witness shamans telling fortunes on the street by face-reading. Mantic and magic arts are prominent in Chinese, Korean, and Japanese life. Buddhism and Daoism are important aspects of Asian popular beliefs and work as vehicles for transferring the magical lore of Asia, which is set in a framework of Chinese traditions. There are blurred boundaries between the occult sciences and the concepts of dualism (yin-yang), and of wuxing (earth, fire, metal, water, and wood), similar to the Wiccan connection to the elements. Belief in the magical powers of water, fire, air, earth, and spirit, as well as astrology, numerology, and other occult theoretically based religious beliefs is common among Asian witchcraft practices and other ancient religions. Symbols of the calendar not only mark the passage of time, but also make up the succession of celestials whose powers of magic can be invoked through talisman and spells.

SEIDR/NORSE WITCH

Norse witchcraft is based mainly on medieval texts, such as the Eddas, documented after Christianization. These writings are made of beliefs and stories that were commonly held by Northern Germanic tribes. Norse, Scandinavian or Viking mythology laid the groundwork for the legends and beliefs of the people of Scandinavia, and Norse paganism.

Seidr

Seidr means witchcraft or sorcery in the old Norse language. It involves manipulative magic, called *galdrar*, and divination, usually practiced by women known as *Völva*. There were male *seidrs*, but they were generally held in less esteem. Goddesses of Norse mythology, such as Freya and others, were *seidr* magicians, as was Odin, who was harassed by Loki for practicing it, because it was considered to be unmanly. Freya was Odin's *siedr* teacher.

Völva

A *Völva* was a shaman, priestess, or wise woman in Norse paganism. These priestesses were among the highly respected elites of society, who cared for the physical and spiritual needs of the people by methods of prophecy and herbalism. Some of the literature suggests that *Völva* were persecuted and marginalized during Christianization at the end of the Viking era, but they would carry on in the northern European notion of witch. They are recurring figures in Norse pagan mythology. A *Völva* practiced prophecy, shamanism, sorcery, and other types of indigenous magic. Mythological and historical portrayals of *Völvas* were thought to have such powers that even Odin the God, consulted them for future telling. Early depictions of *Völvas* described them as old women dressed in white who conducted sacrificial rituals on war prisoners, and used sprinkles of their blood to prophesize the future.

GEORGIAN WITCH

Georgia is a country of myths and legends that have been preserved as famous tales. Many of the Georgian folklore merged with biblical legends in the 5th century.

- *Legend of Tbilisi*: Today, Tbilisi is a lush forest where no one has lived since as early as 450 AD. Legend holds that King Vakhtang I Gorgasali of Iberia went into the woods hunting with a falcon by his side. The falcon hunted a pheasant, but in their struggle, both birds fell into the stream. When the King's army located the birds, they had been boiled, as the water was hot. The King was so impressed that he built a city in their honor. The capital of Georgia is Tpili, an old Georgian word meaning "warm."

- *"Fourth glass is of the devil:"* This is a legend about wine. When God was living on the earth, he wanted to make an easier life for those who were cast from heaven and sent to work hard on the earth. After contemplating for a long time, God decided that he would create a drink that would allow humans to take a short trip back to heaven. It was believed that God invited all of the angels, demons, and the devil to the first wine tasting. The wine was liked by everyone, including the devil, but as usual, the devil wanted to compete with God, so he created chacha (a potent alcoholic beverage) and asked God to taste it. After God drank four glasses of chacha, he said "those who drink less than four glasses of chacha will be on my side and those who drink four or more, they are on yours." When the Elders of Tianeti drink and feast, they refer to the fourth glass of wine as being "of the devil" and avoid drinking it.

- *St George of Mukhura and Devi (The Giant)*: St. George once lived upon the earth, and he went to the Mukhura village where many Devi (giants) lived. When he wanted to go on a giant hunt, he told his deacon to leave the church doors closed unless the person sticks their little finger through the peephole. This would signal to St. George that he can attack a Devi. When it next happened, the deacon kept the door closed and St. George came running and defeated the giant with great strength. He threw the giant into a ravine and a lake magically appeared. Today, Devi Lake is a place where people go to throw stones into the lake and ask for rain.

SUN WITCHCRAFT

Sun or solar magic can be used anytime, anywhere, by anyone, as long as there is sunshine. From sunrise to sunset and throughout the day, various times have their own strengths, which should be considered when casting spells. For instance, spells that are about new beginnings and fresh starts should be cast at sunrise, while spells for power should be cast at noon, when the sun's power is at full strength. Sun potions, crystals, water, and any other magical objects or tools can be charged and cleansed by basking them in the sunlight.

There is not much of a difference between sun witches and moon witches. It just depends on the time of day that the witch feels drawn to the most or is most comfortable with. Some witches like to draw energy from the elements, like the sun or moon, and others from deities. The sun is usually thought to be a masculine energy, which is important to balancing the moon's feminine energy. Just like being a night owl or a morning person, it is a matter of preference. Not all sun witches are early birds. They can, however, choose the time of day or night to practice according to their intent. Sun witchcraft is outgoing and proactive, while moon witchcraft is much more reserved. Sun magic manifests as power, wealth, and physical energy.

Believe it or not, recognizing a sun witch is easier than you may think. They are more than likely out and about in the sun, getting a tan at high noon. However, remember to protect yourself from the sun if you're looking to tan when sun rays are very strong. They are the people who choose not to sit in the shade when they go to the park. You will often see them turning their faces towards sunshine to feel its maximum effects. They prefer gold more than silver and enjoy warm colors, such as yellow and orange. Their energy is strongest during spring and summer and they are less active during fall and winter.

MOON WITCHCRAFT

Lunar rituals have been practiced since ancient times and are still very much alive today. Ancient Babylon and Egypt worshipped the moon. Present day moon rituals offer you a sacred place for introspection, spreading love, setting intentions, and becoming empowered. The moon is a powerful source of self-love and self-care because it inspires you to question your goals, needs, and magical opportunities. The moon has eight phases; however, most ritual work involves the new moon and the full moon. The moon and the sun move into alignment during a new moon, balancing their feminine and masculine energy. The time corresponds with positive change.

When the moon is full, it is fully feminine and corresponds with intuition and nourishment. This is a time for magical creativity and personal growth. For me, lunar rituals are about listening to my higher-self and giving myself an occasional pat on the back. I cast my best banishing spells during a new moon and my best prosperity spells on a full moon. There really isn't a wrong time for moon rituals. All phases of the moon possess their own intention and meanings. Remember, the moon controls the tides, and two thirds of our bodies are water, so science also plays a part in your moon magic. Making moon blessed potions, and full-moon spiritual bathing are just a couple of ideas for making magic with the moon's help. Steps for moon magic include:

1. Relax your mind. Full moon magic can take place five days before a full moon and five days after a full moon. Think of all of the unnecessary things in your life: habits, shame, biases, failed relationships, and guilt. Release these to the power of the moon.
2. When the moon is full, unplug all of your devices and put your phone away. Take all of your crystals and put them, along with several open containers (preferably made of clear glass) on top of your car or on a table outside. Place an empty bowl there too in case it rains.
3. In purple ink, write down the things that are creating clutter in your life. Then, burn the paper under the full moon with a white candle and set your intention.
4. Use your fully charged items for your spell work. Use your moon blessed water for your plants, pets, and put a few drops in your tub or essential oil diffuser.

STAR WITCHCRAFT

The concept of star magic is as old as time. Medieval writings have intricate details about constellations, stars, and the best timing to pull their influence into your spell crafting, talismans, healing, and other forms of magic. The remnants of this ancient philosophy are

DIFFERENT TYPES OF WITCHCRAFT AND WITCHES

recognized today in the form of birthstones. Most people take pause to stand rapt in awe when stargazing. Many of the deities we worship are star goddesses. Pagans and Wiccans take great interest in the stars because of the plain fact that the pentagram, their religious symbol, is a star. Celebrating the Esbats goes beyond the twinkling point of the stars that hang like veils across the darkness of the sky. You can find your own celestial markers or learn those of the seasons. For me, as vast as the night sky is, it makes me feel oddly at home.

When you begin to work with star magic, try not to feel frustrated if you don't immediately know exactly what you are looking at in the sky. Start with one star, one constellation, and one season at a time. Learn everything you can about it and how to locate it again. Read as much as you can about start correspondences and classical mythology. Draw stellar energy into your spells and rituals and allow their energy to support you in worship, astrology, and everyday living. The simple act of laying on a blanket and staring up at the stars will connect you with your ancestors, as you will see the exact same thing that they saw. It will let you experience the echoes and wonders that have traveled the eons from the people of the far distant past. The stars' energies encapsulate the earth and embrace us in their stellar web. In the grand scheme of things, we are as tiny as a grain of sand, yet we are part of the wonderful and vast universe, and most incredibly, we can draw on the magic of the stars to enhance the quality of our lives.

STORM WITCHCRAFT

The magic of storms is both terrifying and thrilling to harness. Connecting to the power source is the same as weather magic and elemental workings. Harnessing storm magic uses a storm's energy to manifest your intent. You can think of the storm's power as a type of battery. All of the air surrounding you is charged by the storm, including the ground under your feet. The storm holds in its great arms all of the classical elements: earth, wind, water, fire, and spirit. As a witch, you can learn how to connect with the storm and how to infuse your energy with its energy and channel the power of the storm into your spells. You can physically feel the massive energy of a storm coursing through your veins. It is so powerful, that once you learn how to work with it, you don't need any ritual or tools. But do carry an anti-lightning talisman.

Storm magic is untamed and wild, yet neutral. It holds negative and positive energies and can destroy and bless the earth. For this reason, storm magic demands respect. You can work with it, but you can't control it. If your ego ever butts in and you think you can master a storm, your magic will quickly falter, and the storm may strike at you! Hence, you should always have an even temper when approaching a storm. It can feed you energy and it can feed off of your energy. Once I tried to work with a storm after a very rough day at work. The storm lasted three days and left me in a blackout.

If you are new to storm magic, first try meditating during a storm. Sit inside your house with your windows open so you can feel and hear the vibrations of the rain and wind while thinking only of the storm. Pay attention to the living being that is the storm, and breathe its energy in and release it. You will know when the connection takes place, as an energy surge will radiate through you. For some, it is a shiver, for others it is a warmth. Once you are connected, call for a rise in the rain, wind, thunder, or request a lightning flash. Once something you have called for materializes, you are synced with the storm.

DIFFERENT TYPES OF WITCHCRAFT AND WITCHES

TYPE OF STORM	MAGICAL PROPERTIES
Regular rainstorms	Love, friendships, healing, cleansing negative energies.
Heavy windstorms	Addiction recovery, academics, breaking bad habits, sending messages to the dead, wishes, and mental spells.
Snowstorms	Transformational magic, purification, change, renewal, protections, and matters of the heart.
Fire storms. A fire storm happens when the land turns ablaze due to the sun's searing heat getting brushed with the wind.	Power, courage, banishment, oath/commanding spells, and protection. *** USE CAUTION
Storms during an eclipse	These are extremely rare, yet powerful storms, which yield great magical powers. It is believed that an eclipse storm's energy can be harnessed to cure illnesses, banish unwanted spirits or energies, and achieve successful exorcisms.

4

WITCHCRAFT SUPPLIES AND THE WITCH'S COMMON TOOLS

Usually, when people first learn about paganism or Wicca, they run out and buy all sorts of magical tools. After all, the internet and other forms of media tell us to buy everything regardless of whether we need it or not. Try to remember, before you hurry over to Ye Shoppe for Witchy Doodads, that magical tools actually have a purpose. Defining your brand of witchcraft first takes understanding that you are magic and that magic lives within you, in all of us, and in the universe. You have all of the tools necessary inside of you to become the type of witch you want to be. It simply means you are connected to the universe and the world in a way that means not harming them.

SACRED SPACES

For those who follow nature or earth-based religions, magic can happen in its truest sense when manifested in a sacred space. It is a space that is sacred because it is in between the physical plane and the spiritual plane. Be careful when choosing your sacred space. Think about the environment, lighting, and distractions, and use your intuition and creativity when designing your sacred space.

Make it your sacred sanctuary. You can make it outdoors or you can make it indoors, where you can sit quietly in darkness to practice rituals. Alternately, make it where you can be in the sunshine and listen to the sounds of nature.

If you are going to create it in a spare bedroom or a corner of your basement, remove everything from the walls and give it a thorough cleaning, throwing out any clutter. Consider buying a new carpet and applying a fresh coat of paint; make it your own. Think about placing an altar there, with a chair for meditation, some candles, and maybe a few sigil pictures on the wall. Then thoroughly smudge the area. Perform a ritual of dedicating your sacred space to a deity of your liking.

> ***Negative energy I toss you away: In this space you cannot stay***
> ***Negative energy I release thee***
> ***My space is clean***
> ***So mote it be***

ALTARS AND SHRINES

Altars and shrines are magical places for spell work and rituals and can be constructed anywhere you can find the space for them. While many witches and pagans place traditional tools on their shrines and altars, you can use whatever fits your needs and your budget. Just be sure you have everything you need for effective spell work and rituals prior to starting your ceremonies. An altar is not at all difficult to make. If you have a small table you can use, great! If you are going to do a lot of outdoor rituals, you can use a flat rock or an old tree stump. If you live in a smaller place, you can create your altar on a dresser top, a footlocker, or an old chest.

If you want to keep a private altar, you may want to make one that is portable and that you can put away when you are not using it.

Find a nice bag or box to house your tools, and then simply get them out when needed. You can use the same bag as your altar cloth. You can also have altars which are permanent and sit out year-round, or seasonal altars you can change with the turns of the Wheel of the Year. I have two altars, one in my kitchen and one in my bedroom. Some of my friends have ancestral altars, with heirlooms, photos, and even urns of deceased family members or family pets. I still remember seeing my first nature altar, which was lovely. It had a piece of driftwood, two seashells, natural crystals, and other outdoor items that paid tribute to the elements and Mother Earth. Your altar is as unique as your spiritual path, so use it as a sanctuary that holds things close to your heart.

When setting up your altar, you will most likely want to include some magical things, but most of all, you'll want it to be functional. It needs to help you manifest your intentions. Here are the most common things that most traditional pagans and Wiccans include on their altars:

- Symbols of the four classical elements, which are aligned with the four cardinal directions. Use a small bowl of sand or dirt to correspond with earth, in the northern aspect of your altar; an incense cone corresponding with air in the eastern aspect of your altar; a piece of charcoal or a candle corresponding with fire in the southern aspect of your altar; and some blessed water in the western aspect of your altar.
- A Goddess' and a God's candle or candles representing the four cardinal directions. Also ready matches or a lighter for your rituals.
- Your wand or athame (dagger). You will need it for your rituals and spell work.
- Your Book of Shadows for your rituals and to keep track of your spell chants.

- Decorate your altar to celebrate a Sabbat or Esbat.

MAGIC WANDS

Paintings from the Stone Age depict wand-type objects of power that are thought to have belonged to powerful leaders. In present day Britain, government officials carry what is known as the "wand of office" to symbolize their power. Witch's wands are used to direct and channel magical energies that are used to influence, rather than command. They correspond with both fire and air elements that are useful in rituals, spell crafting, and casting circles. The wand is considered to be a masculine apparatus, as does the athame, due to its phallic shape.

The wand works as an extension of the witch's powers, and due to its correspondence with the air element, it is associated with logic, communication, and intellect. They can actually be made from any material you feel attracted to. Mine is made of oak and it has a clear quartz ball on the tip, so I can use both ends when working a spell. I love my wand because it gives me a feeling of connectedness to my magic. I cleanse and charge it every day with a sage smudge and then I put it in between the leaves of my sage plant to charge overnight. It actually emanates an aroma from the plant that I can sense while I am working because I keep it on top of my keyboard for inspiration and technomancy. Historically, willow wands have been used for healing spells.

A lot of witches make their own magic wands as DIY projects because they can use the materials they want to personalize, decorate, and design a wand to direct powers that they feel most connected to. Making your own magic wand allows you to bond with your tool and form a special relationship. A wand on its own isn't magical; it gets its magic from you and can act as one of your main tools for strengthening your intentions.

ATHAME

The athame is used in many pagan and Wiccan magical practices as tools for channeling energy. Oftentimes, it is used to cast a circle. You can use it in any situation when you would use a wand. It is a double-edged dagger and it can be hand-made or purchased at your local metaphysical shop. It is not used for actually cutting things physically. There are also numerous websites that offer guidebooks and instructions on how to handcraft an athame. Athames are thought to symbolize fire, so using your athame to outline your casting circle is like writing it in fire. You also use it to call the powers of the elements into your circle and to scribe symbols in your candles and to write words on your candles or in dirt rituals.

WITCH'S BELL

For hundreds of years, witch's bells have been used to drive away evil spirits. The bell's ringing creates powerful vibrations which are the source of great magic. In my coven, we ring bells at Samhain 40 times and at All Hallows 40 times. It creates harmony in a sacred space and can be rung to end or begin a ritual and to evoke deities. Some witches shake sistrums, or use a ritual singing bowl or rattle. You can ping your bell with your athame, too!

The beautiful healing tone of a witch's bell can have various magical effects. They can banish negative energies and unwanted spirits, draw in positive energy, rid the air of stagnant energy, and attract desired energetic intentions. The bell is both a tool and a symbol for Wiccans everywhere. They also make a lovely sound effect for different types of rituals and can be used to guard your home. You can hang one by your front door.

BESOM

The witch's broom or besom is used literally for sweeping a sacred space before a ritual. It not only cleans the sacred space physically but sweeps away negative energy and unwanted spirits that may have gathered since your last cleaning. It corresponds with the water element, so it acts as a purifier. Some of my witch friends have collections of handmade besoms and besoms from other countries. Some keep besoms everywhere. They're like a coin collection. I like to drizzle cinnamon essential oil on mine during the winter months and tea tree oil in the fall. The magic formula for the traditional besom is a birch twig bundle bound with willow wands (Wiccaliving.com, 2021).

Along with the growing admiration for handfasting ceremonies (an ancient Celtic ritual in which the hands are tied together to symbolize marriage), there is a growing interest among Wiccans and pagans in the concept of a "besom wedding." This is also known as ceremoniously jumping the broom. It originated during slavery times as a wedding custom in the American South.

CANDLES

Candles are a vehicle for transformational energy. When lit, the energy of a candle is transformed by flame and released. The magic consists in placing your intentions into that energy release and then channeling and shaping that energy to fit your desires and needs. Fire in any form is transformative. This is the same as in cooking or smudging. While fire is the driving force in candle magic, the color of the candle, the symbols you carve into it, and the shape of your candle are also significant. Given all of the correspondences, you can use candles according to the type of ritual or spell you are going to cast.

In both Western and Eastern societies, fire has been used to decode messages, interpret events, divine the future, and decipher prophecies. From ancient times to today, the bones of dead animals have been tossed into fires. When the bones crack from the heat, those cracks uncover the intentions of the goddesses and gods, guide the process of decision-making, and can tell your fortune. Indeed, for much of the cultural history of Western societies, fire has represented divinity and was touted with anthropomorphic abilities, such as growing, breathing, feeding, devouring, and finally turning dead as ash.

Candles, in particular, are central to most modern witchcraft practice. This is because they are symbolic of all of the powers of the fire element and they can be procured easily and utilized in a controlled fashion. These all-purpose magical tools not only help to generate magic from intention, but they are also key to marking sacred space. Instead of emphasizing the destructive aspects of fire, candles symbolize its warmer, gentler, and comforting aspects and thus are commonly used in personal wish spells.

Witchcraft is about intention and transformation, your request, your desires, and your wishes manifested into reality. Candles are great communicators of our intentions; they act as bright messengers, carrying our intent into the universe where it can be felt. As the candle slowly burns, it whisks your intentions to the celestial realm. You can enhance your candle magic by adding herbs and infusing their magic with your candle magic to make your intentions clearer and more potent. You can also elevate your candle magic by carving various sigils onto your candle. This makes your intention visible during ritual work. You can also draw symbols on a piece of paper and place it under your candle during spell castings.

Candle Colors	Magical Properties/Day of the Week
Green	Fertility, nature, abundance, and money, *Wednesday*.
Red	Passion, courage, power, and vitality, *Sunday*.
Pink	Romance, compassion, friendship and innocence, *Tuesday*.
Yellow	Travel, success, imagination, creativity and happiness, *Sunday*.
Blue	Patience, truth, fidelity and communication, *Monday, Friday*.
Orange	Justice, creativity, ambition and joy, *Thursday*.
Purple	Spirituality, warding off evil eye, and wisdom, *Saturday*.
Silver	Dreams and intuition, *Monday*.
White	Peace, purity, balance and cleansing, *Monday*.
Black	Learning, grounding, banishment, and protection, *Saturday*.

CAULDRON

The cauldron has been associated with witches and witchcraft for thousands of years. It is a womb-like, feminine vessel that corresponds with the water element. The Celts associated the cauldron with the Cerridwen mythology, which holds prophetic powers. Cerridwen is the keeper of the cauldron of inspiration and knowledge in the Underworld. There are various magical uses for your cauldron:

- Burn candles, incense, sage, or offerings
- Associate it with the deity of your tradition
- Grind herbs for magical purposes
- Fill it with moon blessed water
- Use it for scrying

- Use a separate cast iron cauldron for culinary purposes and season it well.

SALT

Salt has a rich history of warding off malevolent spirits, and newlyweds are traditionally sprinkled with it to ward off bad luck. Salt circles are also used for protection. Mix some burnt sage to make black salt for banishing spells and place some salted lemon water on your altar to cleanse your sacred home and purify your altar. Salt is a known witch detector, because witches don't eat much salt, so if someone at your table complains that the food is too salty, chances are you are dining with a witch. Also, if you borrow salt from someone, don't give it back to them! Give them a cup of sugar instead. In some pagan folklore, it is bad luck to let someone borrow salt, because they may use it to curse you.

Here's how you can use salt:

- Add salt to your witch's bottle for protection.
- Offer salt to the goddesses and gods.
- Use salt for a house cleansing ritual

CHARGING DAILY ITEMS

Charging and cleansing are two different activities. Cleansing removes unwanted or negative energy from your sacred spaces and from your objects. Charging is replacing that negative energy with energy that is beneficial to your intentions. When you surround yourself with only the energy your intentions will allow, your magic is amplified. At a very basic level, your magic is the ability to effect change in your environment. All things are composed of energy. They include people, objects, animals, trees, buildings, and rocks, among others. In your witchcraft, you'll cross paths with many forms of energy as well: elemental energy, spirit guides, deities, your personal energy, the energy in your candles, crystals, plants, essential oils, and the universe's energy itself. Some energies you bring into your environment are helpful, while others are not. For this reason, it is essential to familiarize yourself with the way varying types of energy make you feel so that you can surround yourself with energies that flow with your dreams, desires, goals, and wishes.

Charging

When you charge an item, you are filling it with a particular energy type. Charging can also be referred to as enchanting, empowering, or programming. You can charge a space or an item with whatever your intentions are. How you charge your magical tools depends on what your plans are for using them. Think of it as giving your tools their daily purpose. You can complement the object's own energy with the energy you add to it. For instance, a nail has the energy of being a nail (it's pointed, metallic, and creative), but you can charge it with the intent of making it a carving tool to scribe your candles or spells or to be more creative on one of your DIY projects.

Some items, like crystals, already have purpose, so when you charge your crystals or your candles you are specifying your intent for them. For example, rose quartz corresponds with friendship, so you can assign your rose quartz with a task of enhancing your friendships, building better communication in your relationships, and so on. But take note that even though crystals, candles, and other magical items correspond with certain things, this doesn't mean you can't use them for others. The energy innately belonging to an item only enhances and adds to your magic. Every and any item can be charged with intention. Usually, though, most witches charge those items they plan to use in a spell or ritual or items they are going to wear as a talisman or charm.

Items you can charge

Any object can be charged with your intention. Items commonly charged include:

- Crystals
- Herbs
- Cooking Ware
- Wand
- Soil
- Water
- Beauty Products
- Pens
- Needles
- Nails
- Sachets
- Witch's Bottles
- Candles
- Talismans
- Amulets
- Charms
- Seeds
- Essential Oils
- Jars
- Runes
- Cauldrons

For instance, you may wish to charge a green tourmaline crystal with a confident, happy, and lucky energy so that its vibrations will bring you prosperity. All you have to do is cup the gem in your hands to access its energy. If you are about to cast a certain spell, you may want to charge your candle for success; then when you decide to light it, it will be charged with your intent. You can add even more of a charge by anointing your candles or crystals with oil and herbs. The same holds true for any items you have charged with your intentions. When you are watering your herbs with moon blessed water or carrying a sachet to bring you love, your items will hold their charge until it is needed.

How to Charge an Item

There are various methods for cleansing and charging your items with your intention. To begin, it is always best to cleanse your objects first by smudging with sage. Here are the steps for charging an object:

1. Choose an object. The object you choose depends on your plans for it. You may have a certain tool such as a wand or crystal. Maybe you just want to charge the coffee cup you use each morning, or the pens and pencils you use for your Book of Shadows. The list of items you can charge is endless.

2. Pick a charging method.

- I love to charge my items under a full moon and fill them up with lunar energy. The sun works too. The sun and moon charge and cleanse at the same time. Simply place your items under the moonlight. Full and new moons are the strongest. Focus your intent for a few moments and let them charge.
- Charge with crystals. You can charge your crystals under the moon or various other methods and they will then be able to transfer that charge to other objects. All you have to do is have the crystal and the other items touch each other.

3. Visualizing: Rub your hands together until they feel warm and tingly. Close your eyes and rub them together one more time. Slowly move your hands apart, being careful not to fling them apart, or you'll have to start over. Feel the bubble of energy between your hands. It will feel bouncy and stretchy. Visualize the bubble, while you focus your intent into the item. You can slowly move your hands around the bubble to feel its energy. Speak or chant your intention aloud. Gently visualize pushing your intention into the bubble, and picture it changing color based on that intention (green for money, gold for abundance, silver for protection, pink for friendship, etc.). Now hold the bubble over your object and feel the energy moving from your fingers into the object. After a few moments, picture the item aglow with your intention. Note: Visualization is using all of your senses, not just seeing. Try to let yourself experience the vibration or humming sound of the energy bubble. Maybe the temperature in your hands moves from warm to cool. Maybe your charge has a certain smell or taste. Practice getting to know how each item's charge feels during and after your work.

*Helpful hint*** It doesn't matter which method you use; charging is about the energy of your intention. Visualize the results you desire while you charge your magical ingredients and ritual tools. Holding your items and using tactile connections transfer your power and energy to them. Speaking your intentions aloud expresses your intent and makes your charge stronger. For example, you can say "I charge this pen through the power of the universe to bring creative energy into my life. As it is and should be."

OPENING AND CLOSING A CIRCLE RITUAL

Opening and closing a circle is a method of showing respect and thanking the elements for helping you to draw in their energy and release it. Face north and say out loud "Thank you for your energy, faithful earth; farewell." Next, face west, and release the water element by saying out loud "I bid you farewell, precious water, thank you for your energy." Next, face south, release fire, and say out loud "Thank you powerful fire; I bid you goodbye." End your circle ritual facing north and release the spirit element saying out loud "I am grateful to you, oh wonderful spirit; farewell as I close this circle and release the energy back to the ground."

Step-by-Step Instructions on How to Cast a Circle

1. Smudge your sacred space with sage, sweep it, and make sure it is clean.
2. Place a crystal or candle in each of the four directions. If you are drawing on the spirit element, draw a pentacle in which your candles and crystals mark the five points.
3. Face east and begin naming each element as you move clockwise to each point. "I call upon water, etc."
4. Enter a trance until you are grounded and centered.
5. Form a connection with each of the elements, imagining how each one of them feels around your body: wind blowing, water swishing, etc., until you have named and connected with each of the elements.
6. Complete your circle facing north.
7. Imagine bright light shooting from the soles of your feet into the core of the earth, and then pull back its energy, and say out loud "Under the Spirit of the Goddess, with these five elements, I cast protection within, above, and below this circle."
8. You are now ready for spell work.

5

HERBAL MAGIC FOR WITCHES

My garden is a sacred and magical place, and you can make yours that way, too. There is a wealth of information on the internet and in bookstores devoted to garden magic. Many pagans and Wiccans have chosen earth-based spiritual journeys and often start their magical gardens at the start of spring. The very concept of experiencing the cycle of life, from seed to blossom to harvest, is the very definition of magic itself. There are goddess Gardens, lunar gardens, gardens devoted to healing magic, and many more. It is up to you what your garden will be devoted to!

Initially, there was no difference between medicine and magic. Today, we know that magic works on a spiritual aspect similarly to the way medicine works on the physical aspect. Without ancient European lore, science could never have developed successfully alongside medicine. There is overwhelming evidence supporting the essential role of magic in the origin of modern-day medicine. It's easy to underestimate the healing power of herbs. People have a tendency to go straight to over-the-counter medications for everything from headaches to indigestion. Western cultures, in particular, have been conditioned to take prescription medications and supplements to the point of physical and psychological dependence. The magic of herbs is that the only formula for their creation comes from nature itself. They are found in leaves, stems, flowers, and berries, instead of a prescription pad, and nurtured by the sun, the water, the earth, and everything that is natural in this world. There is nothing like the wonderful world of plant magic.

It is necessary to understand the differences between what magic is today and the role it played in medicine thousands of years ago. Historically, magic was built on the premise that the world was created by God and that all of life was connected in an ongoing chain. Correspondences between beings in one aspect of the chain and creatures or elements elsewhere on this continuous chain all are the purpose of God's creation. Life's *purpose* is the founding belief of magic. Since nature did not create anything by mistake or in vain, there must be a purpose for everything. The belief is that God left hints about correspondences, such as the flesh in a walnut shell resembling the human brain. Everything is connected. The role of the magician was to identify all of the corresponding associations and their exact magical properties, so they could be put to good use.

Similarly to the role played by magic in the history of science, herbal healing is as old as humanity itself. The relationship between humankind and the quest of healing naturally goes back thousands of years. It is noted in the recipes of ancient herbal remedies, historical documents, and monuments dedicated to preserving plants. Through the millennia of using medicinal herbs to fight against disease and illness, humans have continued to use bark, seeds, leaves, fruits, and other plant components as medicine. Modern day pharmacotherapy has acknowledged that medicinal ingredients are active in herbs and now includes them in a variety of medications of plant origin. Each herb has significant and special magical properties, stemming from its roots, petals, flowers, and leaves and can be used for cleansing and charging your magical tools, for healing magic, or for nourishment for your body and soul.

ESSENTIAL HERBS

Cayenne pepper does a lot more than just spice up your chili, and nutmeg has a lot more properties that are underutilized when you're making a delicious eggnog. Your kitchen spices and herbs are filled with magical properties just waiting for you to add your intent. Not only will the following list of commonly used herbs and spices elevate the magic in your spells, but it will also help you to connect your magical side to your spiritual side and use them as a dynamic duo in your everyday life.

ALOE VERA

Aloe vera is actually part of the Lily family, and is related to garlic and onion. The Ancient Egyptians called Aloe Vera "the plant of immortality." The Mesopotamians used aloe vera to protect them from vampires and to ward off evil spirits. This is also seen elsewhere with the use of garlic to protect people from vampires. The Hindus called aloe vera "the silent healer" and thought it to be a holy plant from the Garden of Eden. When I was a youngster and got burned or sunburned, I loved darting off to the backyard for some of that magical sticky gel that would make me feel better. It is a feminine plant corresponding with the moon.

Latin Name: Aloe vera, Aloe barbadensis

Folk Names: Burn plant, the desert lily, and elephant's gall.

Element: Water

Magical Uses: Healing, abundance, beauty, moon magic, protection, and love.

ALLSPICE

Allspice was used by the ancient Mayans as an embalming ingredient for their dead and also by the Arawak to cure meat. It makes a wonderful addition to chocolate, too. Allspice is named so because it highlights the aroma of many different spices, such as nutmeg, cinnamon, pepper, juniper berries, and cloves. It is a well-known remedy for toothaches, works great to freshen your breath, and helps with digestion. It has been used in healing spells for centuries.

Latin Name: P. dioica

Folk Names: Jamaican pepper, pimento

Element: Fire

Magical Uses: Increased energy, luck, determination, money, and mood enhancement.

ANGELICA

Angelica is commonly used by ethnic witches. It is medicinally used for heartburn, dementia, anxiety, fever, insomnia, arthritis, flatulence, nocturia, and a host of other ailments. Since ancient times, angelica has been a powerful healer and guardian of women. It is also kept in a white flannel pouch near a baby's crib to bring good health. It is also noted to cause sunburn when used topically on body parts exposed to sunlight, so wear some sunscreen if you are using angelica on your skin. Angelica is a truly divine herb used to communicate with archangels and the higher realms.

Latin Name: Angelicus

Folk Names: Holy ghost root, archangel root, wild celery

Element: Fire

Magical Uses: Protection, luck, breaking hexes, exorcism, prosperity, healing, and divination.

BASIL

Originally grown over 5,000 years ago in India, basil has become an important element in medicinal, culinary, and magical practices. The word basil comes from the Greek word for "king" and means "fragrant" in English. To the ancient Greeks, basil was associated with great wealth and royalty, hence its meaning. However, it corresponds with love and romance more than wealth and royalty. The association between basil and love is so meaningful that in the past, gentlemen tucked basil into their hats when planning on courting a woman. Next time you come across your love interest, offer a basil sprig to ensure a future relationship. Sprinkle some basil leaves over the heart of your lover and they will always remain faithful.

Latin Name: Ocimum sp.

Folk Names: Witches herb, king's herb

Element: Fire

Magical Uses: Astral projection, hedge riding, peace, love, protection, money, banishment, and purification.

CARAWAY

Caraway is a licorice-like tasting herb from the carrot family that has slight anesthetic characteristics that help soothe an upset stomach. It is an anti-flatulent (carminative), so it makes for a great after-dinner tea. Ancient Germanic people sprinkled caraway in the tombs and coffins of their dead to ward off evil spirits. It is believed that putting some in your car glove compartment or in your wallet will ward off thieves. Folklore has it that when placed under a baby's crib, it keeps negative witchery away, and if mixed into animal feed, it keeps herds of animals together. It is masculine and corresponds with the planet Mercury.

Latin Name: Carum carvi

Folk Names: Meridian fennel and Persian cumin

Element: Air

Magical Uses: Love, protection, energy, memory, spiritual enhancement, money, healing, lust, and fidelity.

GINGER

Yule wouldn't be the same without my favorite magical spice, ginger! Used in gingerbread and ginger tea, this herb became a Christmas staple in the early 1700s. Ginger corresponds with Mars and the Sun. Make some gingerbread cookies, and the world will smile with you. Ginger is a warming, dry, pungent, yang herb used medicinally for illnesses triggered by damp, cold weather in traditional Chinese medicine (TCM). The famous gingerbread man was created by England's Queen Elizabeth I and quickly became a favorite Yuletide treat. In 1907, Canada Dry Ginger Ale was patented by a pharmacist from Canada and became very popular during Prohibition in the U.S.

Latin Name: Zingiber officinale

Folk Names: Ginger, African ginger, Cochin ginger, Jamaican ginger, and Race ginger

Element: Fire

Magical Uses: Grounding, love, creativity, the promise of new beginnings, health, dreams, and money.

CINNAMON

During the 1st Century AD, cinnamon was a pricy spice used for culinary purposes. At that time, cinnamon was worth ten times its weight in silver. When using it for magical purposes, make sure to use real cinnamon, not cassia. It is wonderful as an incense and flavoring for tea. When used in a witch's brew, it elevates your powers and increases clarity. Cinnamon and its warming sensation correspond, obviously, with Yule. I use it to charge and cleanse my besom, as it has antibacterial and antimicrobial properties. It is of the feminine gender and corresponds with Venus or Aphrodite.

Latin Name: Cinnamomum verum

Folk Names: Sweet wood, Ceylon cinnamon

Element: Fire

Magical Uses: Increases high spiritual vibrations, love spells, elevates psychic powers, lust, protection, healing, and money.

MINT

The magic of mint makes it a favorite among witches. It is very easy to grow, but keep it in its own pot or it will take over your garden. There are approximately 20 species of mint. The "Mentha" variety was originally found in the Mediterranean Region, while spearmint originated in Egypt and was taken to Europe during the Crusades. It was used as an "arm plant" by the ancient Romans because they would rub it under their armpits as a deodorant. It was also used by the Romans and Greeks in sauces and holiday festivities. The mint's correspondences come from ancient folklore and have always been associated with deities. Mentha was a nymph who caught the attraction of Hades; soon they became lovers. When Hades chose Persephone over Mentha, she began to harass Persephone, who in turn beat Mentha into dust. Afterward, Hades took the dust and transformed it into a plant, so that Mentha would live forever. It is of the feminine gender and corresponds with planet Mercury and deities Pluto and Hecate.

Latin Name: Mentha piperita, Lamiaceae

Folk Names: Garden mint, peppermint, water mint

Element: Air

Magical Uses: Healing, love, protection, luck, attract good spirits, money, dreams, and banishing spells.

STAR ANISE

Star anise originated in Vietnam and Southern China. It has a rich history, dating back to hundreds of years before Christ. It takes 20 years to produce seeds and is a difficult tree to transplant. It was used in the early 1500s in Europe to flavor puddings, syrups, and jams due to its sweetness. It is also used as a digestive aid in Asia. Shaped as an eight-point star, this spice corresponds with divine information, microcosm and macrocosm, expansion, and stability. Star anise is masculine and corresponds with planet Jupiter, which is associated with Sagittarius and Pisces in astrology.

Latin Name: Illicium verum

Folk Names: Eight Horns, Chinese five spice, Chinese anise, Illicium, Chinese star anise

Element: Air

Magical Uses: Hoodoo, mojo bags, good luck, anxiety, psychic awareness, anointing, purification, and cleansing.

How to Create Magic with Herbs

1. Making your herbs magical aligns their vibrations with your magical intention. Sometimes, you can accomplish this with the use of a single herb or multiple herbs in a blend. Their magic grows by exposure to each other.
2. The best way is to start a collection of herbs from either your own garden or the wild. The store should be your last resort for getting these herbs. Say loudly, "I am gathering these precious herbs for healing, love, prosperity, etc." Next, put them on your altar in a bowl along with corresponding crystals and candles, and start visualizing your desires.
3. Run your fingers gently through the blend of herbs while slowly and softly whispering your intention, for example "Petals of daisy, petals of rose, bless me with a heart that knows."
4. Now enchanted, your herb blend is ready for spell casting, or to be put into mojo jars to place around your sacred spaces. You can infuse rosemary, mint, lavender, and basil in boiling water. Only use Pyrex for this, no metal. Keep a lid on the blend tightly so that no steam escapes. For every cup of boiling water, use one tablespoon of herbs, and strain before consuming. Also place some water in your bathtub, and charge your crystals and other magical items just by placing them next to the bowl.

INCENSE

Any combination of herbal materials mixed together with charcoal makes incense. Burning aromatic herbs and resins is a tradition shared by many cultures and has been for millennia. Not only does incense smell wonderful, but it is also used for purification, cleansing rituals, and healing ceremonies. For magical uses, the vibrational energy of incense is used in spell crafting accompanied by visualization, as well as background vibrations used in healing rituals. Grind your herbs with a pestle and mortar, and mix them with some charcoal in your cauldron, abalone shell, or incense burner. Cast away!

FRANK'S INCENSE RECIPE

I grew and harvested this blend of lavender, rosemary, and lemongrass in my own herbal garden.

Ingredients

- 2 teaspoons of rosemary
- 1 ½ tablespoons of lemongrass
- 3 teaspoons of lavender
- 1 ½ tablespoon water

Steps

1. Using your pestle and mortar, grind your herbs into a fine powder.
2. Mix the herbal powders.
3. Slowly add five drops of water at a time, mashing the powder with a spoon's back without stirring.
4. Form into a dough ball, just barely moist so it holds together.
5. Pinch a small piece of the dough and shape it into a tall and thin cone.
6. Place it on a flat surface and let sit for two weeks.
7. When it's ready, just light the tip of the cone and enjoy it on a fireproof surface.

MAGICAL POWERS OF TREES

The Plant Kingdom awards us with many benefits, such as food, medicine, beauty, the ability to make paper, shelter, and shade. Specifically, the gifts provided by trees are incredible. Trees provide us with oxygen and take in carbon dioxide, providing the air that we breathe. They offer us food in the form of nuts, seeds, fruit, syrups, and berries. Some of my favorite tree foods include bananas, cherries, coconuts, pecans, and apples. Medicinally, the edible parts of trees provide us with antioxidants and anti-inflammatories, as well as other fantastic healing attributes. For example, for 300 million years, Ginkgo biloba fruits have been enhancing capillary circulation in people who use it to help delay their aging process.

Monkeys, birds, racoons, squirrels, and millions of other animals find a home in our trees. Trees are worshipped and respected in every culture and are surrounded by traditions of fertility and wisdom. We have all heard about the Tree of Life in the Garden of Eden. In the Old Testament, there are mentions of the healing properties of trees. The stealthy oak tree was worshipped by the ancient Druids; village elders would meet underneath it to absorb strength and wisdom. The trees' essence is divine and closely connected to humankind because they symbolize the cycle of life. Their seeds represent birth, and their falling leaves represent death, as they decay into compost. Just like our blood flows through our circulatory system, a tree's nutrients flow through its system, traveling from their roots, through their trunk, out to their branches, and back.

There is nothing quite like peak foliage. As the colors change throughout the year, it has an amazing visual effect that elevates our higher self. Suddenly catching the scent of an evergreen tree brings back memories of wonderful family times around the

Christmas table. Just sitting in the shade is relaxing and can be a ritual in itself.

Here is a list of 39 trees and their magical properties:

1. Alder: Protection, resurrection, banishing, healing, and psychic intuition
2. Apple: Love, garden, healing, immortality, and goddess
3. Ash: Communication, healing, love spells, balance, knowledge, transition, fertility, and protection from drowning
4. Aspen: Endurance, peace, success, eloquence, rebirth, ancestry, and astral planes
5. Banyan: Divine connection, luck, protection, abundance, immortality, and longevity
6. Bamboo: Luck, protection, flexibility, fortune, and longevity
7. Beech: Creativity, second sight, ancestry, wisdom, and protection.
8. Birch: Creativity, fertility, healing, love, protection, goddess, inspiration, renewal, and birth.
9. Blackthorn: Strength, truth, protection, and authority
10. Bottlebrush: Energy, love, banishing, purification, and abundance
11. Camphor: Cleansing, exorcism, love, prophecy, dreams, healing, and lust
12. Cedar: Dreams, immortality, prosperity, purification, healing, wisdom, and longevity
13. Cypress: Healing, solace, longevity, protection, and grieving.
14. Driftwood: (This is not actually a tree, but it has been infused with the water and earth elements, so it takes on the magic of the sea and the power of the earth.): intuition, dreams, grounding, moving, and ancestor work

15. Elder: Fairies, healing, protection, sleep, magic, blessings, creativity, and transition
16. Elm: Grounding, intuition, rebirth, healing, wisdom, compassion, and birth
17. Fig: Divination, fertility, love, luck, prosperity, and ancient ancestry
18. Fir: Protection, vitality, prosperity, birth, rebirth, and far-sightedness
19. Gorse: Fertility, protection, prosperity, and divination
20. Hawthorn: Cleansing, fertility, marriage, family, happiness, protection, wisdom, purification, and fairies
21. Hazel: Spirituality, luck, protection, passion, changes, and spirituality
22. Heather: Luck, protection, healing, changes, and spirituality
23. Hemlock: Shadow work, cleansing, and mysteries
24. Hickory: Transformation, flexibility, protection, abundance, kindness, and transformation
25. Holly: Death, healing, protection, courage, rebirth, and unity.
26. Juniper: Healing, protection, love, and cleansing
27. Magnolia: Dreams, clarity, love, protection, and truth
28. Maple: Communication, grounding, money, wisdom, love, and divination
29. Mimosa: Love, purification, happiness, and sensitivity
30. Oak: Fertility, prosperity, strength, success, luck, wisdom, ancestry, and health
31. Palm: Fertility, healing, protection, abundance, and potency
32. Pine: Emotions, luck, love, purification, protection, emotions, healing, immortality, and regeneration
33. Rowan: Expression, grounding, luck, protection, fertility, centering, strength, and writing
34. Sequoia: Eternity, wisdom, enlightenment, growth, and valor

35. Spruce: Enlightenment, versatility, healing, grounding, protection, and intuition
36. Willow: Motherhood, protection, wishes, healing, fertility, knowledge, relationships, intuition, relationships, and flexibility
37. Witch Hazel: Healing and protection
38. Yew: Strength, flexibility, rebirth, divination, ancestry, and death

MAGICAL POWER OF FLOWERS

Flowers are manifestations of divine wisdom and beauty. Every flower has its own unique vibrational energy. Flowers are universal in their expression and they are readily available as a gift to us all. Flower magic means using a flower to focus our attention upon in order to manifest our positive desired change. The flowers that nature provides have been used in magic for centuries. Mother Earth is one of our connections to the universe and provides us with the ability to ground ourselves. Ritual adds structure, ceremony, and a certain excitement to everyday life, transforming the mundane into magic and the boring into the extraordinary.

Using Flowers on the Altar

At the center of our ritual and other magical practices is our altar. Using flowers to honor our magic is a beautiful way to focus and hold our intention. Placing those flowers on our altars illuminates our intentions. There is so much beauty in the presentation of a bouquet or collection of flowers that is specifically chosen for its energy and the meaning it brings to any ritual. Flower symbolism is an important part of how your desires manifest. Do not collect flowers randomly when you wish to use them as part of a ritual. Collectively or individually they highlight the desire and intentions behind the ritual itself.

Flower	Magical Uses
African Daisy	Mystique, protection, fine-tuning energy fields, divinity, healing, and magical powers
Agapanthus	Authority, excellence, self-love, intelligence, intuition, confidence, self-mastery, and divinity
Alyssum	Comfort, peace, grounding, immunity, healing, staying true to yourself, and gentleness
Bird of Paradise	Self-awareness, recognizing invisible entities, insight, protection, sacred geometry, astral traveling, interconnectedness, and math
Bleeding Heart	Finding the beauty in pain, healing, love, emotions, depression, sexuality
Camellia	Alignment with the Goddess, confidence, authenticity, decision making, humility, prosperity, and receptivity
Carnation	Beauty, rebirth, love, healing a broken heart, longevity, and vigor
Chamomile	Breaking hexes, protecting children and animals, harmony, sleep, peace, prosperity, and soothing
Dahlia	Dreams, shadow talk, occult knowledge, and emotional transmutation
Daisy	Health, wealth, purification, and simplicity
Dandelion	Animal healing and protection, happiness, wishes, and divination
Echinacea	Health, service, fortification, support for those in the helping or healthcare industries, joy, and heartiness
Freesia	Clarity, transmutation, healing after birthing, depression, courage, and removal of blocked chakras

Flower	Magical Uses
Heather	Ancestral connections and wisdom, luck, healing (physical and emotional), memory, protection, and transmutation
Impatiens	Divine timing alignment, grounding, and being present
Jasmine	Abundance, relaxations, attract love, joy, relaxation, and sexual energy
Kalanchoe	Grounding, protection, resilience, inner-strength, and harmony
Lavender	Clarity, joy, protection, balance, harmony, stress reduction, mend a broken heart, relaxation, healing relationships, and releasing shame and guilt
Magnolia	Ancient knowledge, Goddess energy, independence, personal growth, fidelity, wonderment, and awe
Narcissus (Daffodil)	Astral travel, mindfulness, romance, freedom from being stuck in the past, spirituality, and self-love
Orchid	Elegance, uniqueness, royalty, orgasm, fertility, wealth, love, beauty, harmony, intuition, and luxury
Poppy	Calmness, connection to deities, beating addictions, peaceful death, relaxation, sleep, release, and surrender
Rose	Abundance, love and romance, dreams, blessings, self-love, spirituality, protection, and secrecy
Sunflower	Happiness, vitality, potency, radiance, truth, strength, power, and sustenance
Tulip	Beauty, grounding, alignment with Goddess of love, simplicity, gratitude, heart health, and desire
Ylang Ylang	Joy, sex, peace, positivity, healing, and relaxation

FRANK'S ROSE PETAL BEAUTY LOTION

Roses are a midsummer classic and one of our most treasured scents. Romantic, gentle, and divine, roses are great for nourishing and hydrating our skin and are especially helpful for dry or mature skin. Make the most out of their beautiful abundance by designing your own fragrance skincare products, using organic ingredients to get that rose-smelling velvety feeling all over your body.

Designing a lotion is a bit tricky because you have to combine water and oil, which need an emulsifier. But it only takes three ingredients to make this hydrating rose scented lotion, perfect after an afternoon outdoors, after exercise, or before bed.

Ingredients

- Oil
- Beeswax
- Rose petals

1. Simmer 7 stems of rose petals in distilled water for thirty minutes.
2. Heat 50 ml coconut or shea butter oil with 5 g beeswax in the top of a double boiler.
3. Once your oil and beeswax are melted, pour 3 tablespoons, one tablespoon at a time, stirring constantly.
4. Put cold water on the bottom of your double broiler and stir continuously until the consistency changes.
5. Scoop into a jar and allow to fully cool before covering.
6. Cover and refrigerate.
7. Apply frequently and enjoy!

Charged Floral Water

Charge your floral water under the sun or moon, place it on a windowsill, or surround it with lit tea candles on your altar.

Flower Petal Ritual Bath

Spiritual bathing is a sacred activity. Sometimes, it's the only chance you have during a crazy day to unwind naturally. I have turned my bathroom into a spiritual sanctuary, surrounding the tub with flowers, crystals, candles, and incense. Bathing has been a sacred healing ritual in many cultures spanning the course of history. These sacred bathing rituals have grown since the ancient times when water has always been recognized as an elemental and powerful healing source. People in India, for example, travel thousands of miles to bathe in the sacred energy of water and to seek healing.

In this spiritual bathing ritual, my hope for you is that you will find the inspiration to add a blessed healing aspect to your routine bathing. It is important for both you and your magic to spend some time showing yourself some love.

1. Cleanse the bathroom

Begin this ritual by cleaning and smudging your bathroom and all of your sacred ingredients. Did you know that smudging with sage or Palo Santo acts as an air purifier and reduces the amount of bacteria in the air by 90 percent?

2. Add beauty to your sacred space

After smudging, create a relaxing ambience by lighting a candle and adding some flowers to your bath so that they are in your line vision during the ritual. This provides a spiritual focal point, allowing you to dip into your meditative place. I sometimes just look at the flowers while I am bathing and intimately absorb their natural beauty and my connection to Mother Earth. Add some lavender or rose petals or petals of your flowers of choice to the water or add a muslin bag of dried flower petals to the bath for a floral infusion.

3. Connect to scent

Use a diffuser or other type of burning oil to elevate your senses. Again, rose oil or lavender are perfect for this step. While meditating, visualize the particles of scent traveling through your body and into your heart chakra. Picture a rose in your heart area slowly blooming with the aroma. You can also enjoy some extra mojo by adding a tablespoon of pink Himalayan or Epsom salts. Salt water is naturally healing and a great way to detox your skin.

4. Place a rose quartz crystal around the edges of your tub

You can also put some stones right into the bath water and visualize their healing energy nurturing, loving, and calming you.

5. Finish by expressing gratitude

Mindfully correspond with all of the sacred objects, enveloping yourself with the warmth of the water. Take the time to express your gratitude to each of them for supporting you.

STEP BY STEP GUIDE TO RITUALS AND CRAFTING SPELLS

While it is perfectly okay to use the spells of others and in fact, there is a whole industry devoted to them, there are often times why you will want to craft your own spells. Sometimes, we just get the feeling of needing something personal and original. It is not as difficult as you may think because it is all about your intention.

INTENTION

Rituals and crafting spells have everything to do with intention. They are about making a decision about how you want your intention to manifest by casting a spell. It is essential to let the universe or deities know your exact intention. Remember, you are creating magic with the other powers that be. Also, you don't want to mistakenly manifest the wrong intention. The power of your spells comes from your thoughts and feelings. When you know your intention, you can harness the power you need to make magic happen.

Setting a strong and clear intention prior to beginning your spell is the best way to power it up. After all, it is the intention of the witch that makes or breaks the spell! Here is a simple formula for the beginner or intermediate witch to try:

1. A specific desire (precisely) + the amount of time you want it to be revealed = your intention.

- Using the word "I" and present tense verbs, write down your intention, as if it has already happened.
- Try it out with the following rituals:

2. Journal Ritual: Carve your intention into a candle and light it. While sitting in a sacred place with no distractions, start writing down what your life is like currently.

- Write down your intention

3. Ritual Meditation with Spiritual Correspondence

- Sit quietly in a calm state with your eyes closed.
- Decide with whom you are communicating:

i. The Triple Goddess

ii. The Great Horned God

iii. The universe

iv. The elements (air, fire, earth, water, spirit)

v. Your intuition

vi. Aloud, ask your higher power "What is my want?"

vii. Now listen. Pay close attention to any sounds, sights, tastes, and smells. Your higher self will connect to your spirit guide.

4. Visualize Your Intention

- Meditate on how your life has changed as if it has already happened. Visualize the exact scenarios and make any necessary adjustments.

INVOCATION OF HECATE (THE GODDESS OF WITCHCRAFT)

Hecate is the goddess of magic, sorcery, ghosts, and the spirit world. Early in her reign, she was often invoked when childbirth occurred and for the rites of puberty. Often, she is the known protector of the vulnerable, including children, hunters, shepherds, and warriors. However, she is not protective, nurturing, or motherly. Instead, Goddess Hecate will bring vengeance onto people who have harmed those she protects. In classical Greek times, sacrifices were offered in Hecate's honor, ranging from eggs and cakes to dog meat. She can be invoked to exact divine retribution on those who deserve punishment for their wrongdoings.

Wiccans and pagans, today, honor Hecate as a dark goddess, but that is due to her correspondence to the dark moon, the spirit world, ghosts, and magic. She is not easily invoked. November 30 is the date to honor Hecate. It is known as the Night of the Crossroads (Wigington, 2019). The following are ways you can honor Hecate in your own practices of magic:

1. Stroll down a dark road at nighttime, offering hymns and prayers to Hecate, and wait for her presence.
2. Dogs are most sacred to Hecate, so volunteer at an animal shelter or adopt a dog.
3. Tend to a neglected or deserted place that everyone else has abandoned.
4. Use torches in your rituals, not flashlights. In many art

pieces depicting the Goddess of Witchcraft, Hecate is carrying a fire torch. It is a great way to intensify your magic and to welcome her spirit.
5. Dedicate your altar to Hecate.
6. Yew is known to be sacred to Hecate. Plant it on the boundaries of your property to invite her protection and favor. Be aware, however, that yew is toxic to animals and people.
7. Walk to the point where two roads cross and become one. Burn a black candle there and call upon Hecate to choose the right path or to give a message to a loved one who has passed on.

CRYSTAL MAGIC

Crystals are extremely powerful and surprisingly versatile magical tools. Modern magic practitioners use crystals for divination, healing, prosperity, aligning chakras, love, and much more. Each crystal has its own unique chemical composition and its own magical vibrational signature. Classified as inorganic matter, crystals are thought to be alive because of their healing abilities for all living things. Electrical charges are visible to the naked eye when tourmaline crystals and others are hit with a hammer. This is clear evidence of their innate powers and energies. For witches, the powers of crystals are the same as the powers of nature or the elements. Since our thoughts and intentions are also energy forms, we can use crystals as magical channels to send healing powers and positive energies into the universe. These energies then come back through the spiritual realm and bring positive vibrations and healing powers that manifest actual change in our lives.

Connecting on a personal level with your gemstones is essential when working with them. Learning how to recognize and feel the vibrational energies of your crystals is how you initiate and strengthen your connection. As previously discussed, you can cleanse and charge your crystals with moonlight, sunlight, dirt, sage, water, and palo santo. If you do not feel the energy of your crystals when holding them in your hands, don't worry; eventually, practice will teach you how powerful they really are.

Here are some quick tips to "raise your vibes" and sense their energy:

1. Set aside predetermined notions.
2. Remove any gemstone jewelry (including any wedding and engagement rings). You will be able to palpate the vibrational energy of your crystal better if there is no interference from other stones.
3. Unplug all distractions, such as smart devices, TV, radios, etc.
4. Pick a stone you feel an attraction to.
5. Your own vibrational frequencies will resonate with the crystal you feel attracted to.
6. Spend a few moments in a trance before picking up your crystal.
7. Practicing some deep breathing will help you to focus and visualize the crystal's energy with each deep breath. Imagine the glow around the crystal when you exhale.
8. Rub your hands together until they feel warm to align the energy centers in your palms with the stone.
9. Put the stone in the hand you feel is drawn to the stone or in your non-dominant hand.
10. Spend a few moments focusing on the energy of the crystal. While zeroing in on the stone, pay close attention to any physical sensations in your hands or anywhere else in your body (such as feet, arms, or head). Take note of any emotions you feel as well.
11. Pay attention to the temperature of your hands while

holding your crystal. Can you feel any vibrations, trembling, or buzzing? Do you feel any tingling sensations, chills, or goosebumps? If you feel any of these sensations, or really any sensation at all, you are picking up the vibrational energy of the crystal.
12. As you inhale and exhale, imagine the crystal's energy taking form, allowing it to grow with each breath.
13. As you breathe in, take the crystal's healing energy into your body and through every cell of it.
14. As you exhale, gently share the energy with the universe.
15. Without forcing anything, allow your gem to carry you on a serene journey where your body is encapsulated in its healing light.
16. Thank your crystal aloud.

MEDITATION

Meditation is a way to slip into silence and take a break from the noises of the outside world and inner turmoil, while tapping into the spiritual realm and total relaxation. There are many mental, spiritual, emotional, and physical benefits to meditation. It reduces your stress levels, relieves pain, and helps you to connect to your inner witch, improving your magical prowess. Meditation enhances your insight, giving you the know-how to communicate with gods and goddesses and the elements. Magic practitioners use meditation as a tool in preparation for rituals, divination, and spell crafting. The two main methods of meditation include concentrating on your breathing, a single mantra, and mindfulness, which is aligning yourself with the universe and all that is sacred. It amounts to training your thought processes to acknowledge every sense, perception, and thought passing through your mind without getting stuck on a single one. Here is a step-by-step method for concentration meditation:

1. Sit or lay in a relaxed position with your eyes closed while wearing comfortable clothing.
2. Concentrate on inhaling and exhaling, feeling the sensations of each breath.
3. If you start to feel distracted, slowly restructure your thinking without self-judgment.
4. Recite prayers, sounds, words, or whispers, such as humming or affirmations.

MINDFULNESS

Mindfulness is a skill derived from the practice of being present in the presence of the universe and in the current moment. It means getting the most out of each second that life has to offer, rather than consuming your mind with worries about the past or the future. Sometimes, letting go of what can go wrong, what has gone wrong, and how things would be if you had done things differently seems impossible. But it can be done.

Mindfulness is a survival mechanism, which allows people to be consciously aware of any approaching predators and prey. It makes use of all senses to ensure safety. In the modern world, mindfulness can help us feel happy and centered in a world full of chaos. It gives us a way to manage intrusive, negative, and ruminating thoughts. In spite of our wishes, life happens, and mindfulness is the practice of training your mind to react in such a way that it will benefit your health and wellbeing the most.

Modern witchcraft has one simple premise. Your thoughts matter. Whether they are good thoughts or bad, whatever you focus your thoughts on will manifest in your life. This is also known as the Law of Attraction. We all know those people who seem to always have a storm cloud following them around. They seem to be addicted to chaos and conflicts. Well, the opposite of that is also true. People who think positively tend to attract other positive thinkers. They seem to be the lucky ones and are able to gracefully navigate through the difficult times in life.

Mindfulness is the grounding force behind modern witchcraft. Regardless of whether you're a magical tool collector, soloist, or minimalist, this part of the craft is often the most neglected. Worrying about things that happened twenty years ago or where you'll be tomorrow leaves out living today. There are always going to be issues outside of what you can control, but accepting your experiences is a far cry from playing victim or being the VIP of your pity party. Feeling shame and guilt over things from the past is like carrying a huge weight on your shoulders everywhere you go.

When it comes to being a mindful witch, it boils down to staying present and controlling your thoughts. Try starting your day with a magical morning ritual. Set your intentions for the day, including when you will meditate, exercise, call upon the elements, and converse with your spirit guides.

Meditation is the key element to practicing mindfulness, so try the following ritual. On a full moon night, find a quiet and relaxing sacred space outside, hopefully in a natural setting, where the full moon is in your line of sight. If distractions interrupt your focus, imagine soaking the moon's energy through your mind's eye. Imagine the moonlight filling your body with a soothing brightness and mental clarity. Also try to mindfully watch the sunrise or focus on the aroma and taste of your morning cup of coffee and bring yourself into a state of peacefulness.

The goal of meditation and mindfulness is not so much to control what happens to you physically, as it is to control your thoughts. Controlling your thoughts through meditation and mindfulness will also improve your overall situation in the long run. This is the heart of modern magic.

FINAL THOUGHTS

Remember that magic is a skill set, a tool, and a way of life, but using your common sense should also be a factor. You can cast 1,000 spells for getting a new job, but if you don't get out there and pound the pavement and send out your resumes, your chances of finding that job are greatly reduced.

Everyday life has become digital and fast-paced, which can separate you completely from the natural order of things and the spiritual realm. The aim of this book was to show you how to practice self-love in spirit, body, and mind by learning and then integrating the ancient practices and philosophies of paganism and Wicca, the oldest known religion in human existence.

Wicca and paganism are nature-based religions that hold a common belief in the union of spirit, nature, and being. Pagans and Wiccans come from every ethnicity, cultural background, socio-economic status, sexual orientation, gender, and walk of life. The pagan lifestyle, including Wicca, is a beautiful existence that promotes a relationship with the celestial realm, inner peace, and powerful ways to commune with the elements and all that is the universe.

FINAL THOUGHTS

We have talked about the history of trees, herbs, flowers, and plant magic so as to offer you a guide for your unique interpretation of natural and herbal magic. You should now be able to integrate them into your everyday life, while manifesting a spiritual environment to work with and practice your craft. Plants and trees, coupled with crystals, candles, and essential oils, are essential components of witchcraft. A charm, potion, spell, or ritual is only as good as the ingredients you incorporate into it. Many individuals use crystal and herbal magic for astral projection, increasing spiritual energy, aligning their chakras, giving offerings, and powering up their spells.

Spiritual energy is a life force that exists everywhere. It exists in the celestial realm, in empty spaces, within the smallest of molecules, and throughout galaxies. You can raise your spiritual energy by practicing mindfulness and owning a sense of inner peace. The union of peace, love, and joy is what empowers and strengthens your vibrational energies. It is important to keep in consideration that the static and noise surrounding us can interfere with our connections to the deities. Spirit guides are macrocosmic forces with a strong desire to help. Limiting the noise and the use of technology can help you to experience the fullness of life and open doors to wonderful opportunities if you are able and willing to be present in the moment.

I hope that you enjoy this book as much as I loved writing it. If you do, it would be wonderful if you could take a short minute and leave a review on Amazon as soon as you can, as your kind feedback is much appreciated and so very important. Thank you.

SOURCES

Chevalier, G., Patel, S., Weiss L, Chopra D, & Mills PJ. (2019).The effects of grounding (Earthing) on bodyworkers' pain and overall quality of life: A randomized controlled trial. *Explore (NY)*15(3):181-190. doi: 10.1016/j.explore.2018.10.001. Epub 2018 Oct 11. PMID: 30448083.

Doyle, E. (2016). Wicca: History, belief, and community in modern Pagan Witchcraft. *Brighton, Chicago, and Toronto: Sussex Academic Press.* ISBN 978-1-84519-754-4.

Fra. A.o.C. (2002). *A short treatise on the history, culture and practices of The Hermetic Order of the Golden Dawn.* https://web.archive.org/web/20070928121719/http://www.osogd.org/library/biscuits/history.html

Grimassi, R. (2000). Encyclopedia of Wicca & Witchcraft. *Llewellyn Publications.* ISBN 1-56718-257-7, ISBN 978-1-56718-257-

Guiley, R. (2008). Church and School of Wicca". *The Encyclopedia of Witches, Witchcraft and Wicca* (third ed.). New York: Checkmark Books. pp. 61–62. ISBN 978-0816071043.

Nautiyal, C., Chauhan, P., & Nene, Y. (2007). Medicinal smoke can completely eliminate diverse plant and human pathogenic bacteria of the air within confined space. *J Ethnopharmacol. 3;114*(3):446-51. Epub 2007 Aug 28. PMID: 17913417

Llewellyn Encyclopedia. (2008). Golden Dawn. *Timeline*. https://www.llewellyn.com/encyclopedia/article/35

Oschman, J. L., Chevalier, G., & Brown, R. (2015). The effects of grounding (earthing) on inflammation, the immune response, wound healing, and prevention and treatment of chronic inflammatory and autoimmune diseases. *Journal of inflammation research, 8,* 83–96. https://doi.org/10.2147/JIR.S69656

Stardust, L. (2021). How to use technomancy as a protection spell for your phone. *Teen Vogue*. https://www.teenvogue.com/story/how-to-use-technomancy

Wigington, P. (2019). Alexandrian Wicca. *Learn Religions*. learnreligions.com/alexandrian-wicca-2562902.

Wigington, P. (2020). American witchcraft laws. *Learn Religions*. learnreligions.com/american-witchcraft-laws-2562884.

www.ingramcontent.com/pod-product-compliance
Lightning Source LLC
Chambersburg PA
CBHW071420070526
44578CB00003B/626